THE COSTUMES OF

DOWNTON ABBEY

THE COSTUMES OF

DOWNTON ABBEY

EMMA MARRIOTT

weldon**owen**

CONTENTS

INTRODUCTION

The fictional lives of the aristocratic Crawley family and their loyal servants have long enthralled audiences across the globe. The bygone era depicted in *Downton Abbey* is brought to life with an array of captivating characters, all of whom look and seem entirely credible. Brilliantly crafted scripts are key, as are stellar performances by the cast, but costumes have always had an important part to play in the storytelling, the authenticity, and the visual splendor of the series. Indeed, for some fans, the costumes have been the main draw, as they feast upon the elegance and opulence of the Edwardian era through to the vibrancy of the late 1920s.

The drama opens in 1912, when the British aristocracy was at its height and the styles of dress at their most sumptuous. For modern audiences it's a fascinating time—the hats are large and ornate, the gowns floor-length and exquisite, and the men are in tweeds, morning coats, and white tie, while liveried footmen and servants attend to their every need. With that elegance came formality: the Crawleys change several times a day, their lives governed by complex dress codes they couldn't manage without valets, lady's maids, and a household of servants. It is a world riven by social hierarchy, in which etiquette and manners matter—how one behaved and looked reflected where a person belonged, whether they were an earl or a kitchen maid.

By season two, the world erupts into war—the Great War of 1914–18—and we witness the effect that has on the household of Downton Abbey and the rapidly changing world in subsequent years. While the Edwardian era seems distantly removed from modern life, elements start to creep in that feel more familiar. Downton Abbey is wired for electricity, a sewing machine is delivered downstairs, a telephone and wireless installed upstairs, and Edith, Sybil, and Mary begin to explore the new opportunities opening up for women in the postwar years.

In tandem, the fashions in clothing change; the likes of Violet Crawley and Mrs. Hughes remain firmly wedded to their corsets and Edwardian silhouette, but others embrace the new styles. Mary at first rides sidesaddle, donning long skirts and a top hat when she goes out in the hunt, but by season six, she is sitting astride a horse, in jodhpurs and a neat bowler. During the war, we see Edith in breeches and jodhpurs as a land girl and Sybil tending to the injured as a Red Cross nurse, while the men of the household wear service uniforms, with Thomas Barrow swapping the stiff collars of a footman's livery for the khaki tunic of the army and Lord Grantham resplendent in his mess uniform and regiment regalia.

As the years progress, skirt hemlines continue to creep up toward the knee until by 1927 they are at their highest and they start to come down again. A growing interest in dancing and the advent of jazz music inspire new and freer modes of dress, while a straighter, more boyish silhouette becomes popular as waists drop or disappear altogether, with corsets either abandoned or contracted in length. At the same time, dresses begin to be seen in bold colors and printed, textured fabrics, with oriental influences evident in exotic and more fluid garments, jeweled headbands, turbans, and kimonos.

Fashions were at their most daring in the cities, and in London, Edith, Rose, and Mary can really make an impact as they head to galleries and restaurants free from the disapproving air of their family. The changes in fashion, however, are evident at Downton too. Cora still visits her couture designers and dresses in the latest styles, and many of the downstairs staff are interested in the new trends. Daisy and Anna have their hair cut into neat bobs, their uniforms have higher hems and dropped waists,

Opposite: The Crawley sisters in Edwardian-style gowns. By the 1920s (below), the fashion has moved on considerably although long evening gloves are still a must.

and everyone is in awe of the dazzling fashions on show when Hollywood stars visit the house in the movie *Downton Abbey: A New Era*.

Men's fashion also evolves, albeit more slowly: cravats give way to ties, stiff upturned collars to a downturned style or soft collars on the younger gents, wristwatches replace pocket watches, and the tailoring of suits changes considerably. At large houses like Downton, white tie and tails are still required in the evening, although the dinner jacket, or tuxedo, is starting to become a more common sight. Tweed suits and plus fours are still de rigueur for shooting and fishing on the Downton estate, and the hunt retains a complex dress code. Elsewhere, however, new sporting attire emerges: We see Henry Talbot in his racing gear, complete with leather cap and goggles, as society embraces the exciting new world of motorsports. Sportswear emerges in the 1920s, and in *A New Era*, we see Edith, Bertie, Thomas, and Lucy in their tennis gear, looking every inch the bright young things.

For the women in *Downton*, it's not all about partying, and some of the most iconic looks in the series showcase the evolving styles of workwear for women. Edith at her magazine office in London dons some stylish blouse-and-skirt ensembles, while Mary as estate manager at Downton embraces the more androgynous style of three-piece suits, ties, and a cloche hat, a look that she pulls off with predictable flair.

While many of the changing styles of the era are showcased in *Downton Abbey*—and featured in this book—the principal aim of the costumes and of the designers who create them is that they work seamlessly within the drama; they shouldn't take center stage unless, of course, the storyline dictates otherwise. Lady Sybil's turquoise pantaloons in season one are meant to be a shocking sight for both the family and the viewer, but for the most part, costumes should weave into the storytelling without distracting from it.

In fact, a costume can serve a multitude of purposes in a drama, signaling the identity and emotional state of a character, as well as the "where and when" of a story, before a word of dialogue is spoken. If we see Mr. Bates dressing Lord Grantham in a tweed jacket and tie, then it's probably morning time and Robert is heading out to the estate. If Lady Edith slumps down on a sofa in a daring halter-neck dress and beaded headpiece, she's in London and she's had an exciting night out. Lighting, props, and a myriad of elements play their part, of course, but a costume can help to anchor a character into the setting, and can visually speak volumes. A large, plumed hat on Violet serves to emphasize her indignation. Whether it's a starched shirt, a tiara, or brass buttons on a waistcoat, the details can help to set the mood of a scene.

Alongside dressing individual characters, costume designers must also take into consideration the setting of a scene and its visual

Henry Talbot is passionate about racing cars and looks like a twentieth-century man in his white coveralls, racing cap, goggles, and leather gloves.

impact. From the candlelit dining room of Downton Abbey to the village cricket green, they need to carefully plan the overall palette of costumes within each scene and its impact on camera. Evening dinners call for glinting tiaras, white tie, and shimmering beaded dresses; a garden party, creams, linens, and wide-brimmed hats, with everything in frame working together. Isobel and Violet might have dresses in complementary tones, or the decision might be to dress characters in contrasting looks, with Lady Mary in bold geometric patterns while her grandmother is in muted, almost fading colors to reflect their age, emotional state, or where the drama is heading.

Costume designers also need to ensure that key players in a scene, on whom the drama or dialogue is centered, have appropriate impact, even if they are surrounded by a crowd. To do this, they might begin with the key player of the scene, perhaps dressing the actor in a vivid color, before then designing for the surrounding characters or crowd. Downton Abbey also has a very large ensemble cast, and over the years, the costume team, along with hair and makeup, have tried to ensure that characters have instantly recognizable looks and silhouettes, so a viewer can quickly identify, sometimes even from the back of a head, each character. If we see a woman in a long Edwardian dress with keys hanging from a chain, then it's a fair bet it's Mrs. Hughes, the housekeeper. And the silhouette of a tall, elegant female with a sharp shingle bob and tweed suit has all the hallmarks of Lady Mary.

The costume department, like the whole team working on Downton Abbey, are also incredibly detailed in their work, and will add trims, beading, or small items of jewelry specifically to work within the setting of a scene, pairing a gold trim, for example, with the opulent surrounding of the Ritz restaurant in London or similar. They must also consider which type of fabrics and patterns will work on camera, knowing that the high-definition cameras will pick up on the tiniest details, or that colors can look quite different on the big or small screen compared with how they look on a hanger in a vintage shop.

Overseeing the whole process and all the costumes in Downton Abbey is the costume designer, who, aided by a team, sets the look and style of the entire ensemble cast and supporting artists. It's a momentous task involving extensive liaison with the director, producers, production design, hair and makeup, and the entire creative team, and to date, four designers have taken on the role across six seasons and two films. They must immerse themselves in the period styles and recreate them as authentically as possible while also serving the drama of the series and the highs and lows of all the characters.

Initially taking on the role was Susannah Buxton, a multi-award-winning costume designer with experience across film and television, including an Emmy for her work on Downton Abbey. The series was a unique project because, unlike most period dramas, which are based on books or classic stories, Downton Abbey was entirely new, with a large number of characters unknown to the wider world. Susannah therefore had to establish the look of each character, which up until then had appeared only in Julian Fellowes's scripts, a challenge that she relished: "When you're in at the beginning of a series, the excitement is huge, and to have totally new characters was a fascinating experience. Costume designers meet the principal artists soon after they are cast, to show them initial design ideas and to learn their response to the character. We are then able to work on a color palette for them and to take detailed measurements for use in further fittings."

Prior to fittings, costume designers immerse themselves in research, visiting museums and poring over photo collections and books, before working up mood boards of useful imagery and references. Susannah was also excited to explore the fashion of the prewar years, a time that had rarely been depicted in previous dramas, which focused on either the early Edwardian period (the first decade of the twentieth century) or the First World War. Downton Abbey starts two years after George V has succeeded his father, Edward VII, as king and two years before the outbreak of war. Susannah was able to examine the many visual references and photographs from the era, which included fashion magazines, paintings and portraits by such artists as Sargent and Matisse, and, of course, imagery from the Titanic, which famously sank in 1912 and forms an integral part of Downton Abbey's early storyline when Lord Grantham's heir, Patrick Crawley, is killed.

"The year 1912 was a really interesting time in fashion," explains Susannah. "The aristocracy have access to fashion magazines and the French couture designers, but we're also coming out of the very restricted, highly corseted look of the Edwardian period. Encouraged by the likes of fashion designer Paul Poiret, the new silhouette is straighter, with more comfortable corsets, long, slim skirts, little boots, and these great big hats—and then of course the war changed everything again."

Susannah went on to establish all the characters, starting first with the Dowager Countess of Grantham, whom she partly modeled on the then Queen Mary, although she chose to dress Violet in purples,

Mrs. Hughes is usually seen in her dark-colored housekeeper's uniform, with keys and a small pair of scissors hanging from her belted waist.

blacks, and strong greens rather than the pastels and pale colors popular in the Edwardian period.

For season two, Rosalind Ebbutt joined the costume team to oversee and design all the uniforms for the First World War, while Susannah designed many of the principals and the Christmas episode. An award-winning and Emmy-nominated designer, Rosalind, who also has a background in theater and opera, has worked extensively in TV and film, including as a designer for many wartime adaptations. For season two, Rosalind oversaw the trench warfare footage, a large mess dinner in the dining room of Downton, and the conversion of the house into a convalescent hospital for soldiers, along with the hundreds of other scenes that make up a *Downton* season. Susannah particularly enjoyed dressing Edith in her land girl breeches, and she also worked hard to ensure Mary, Cora, and the women upstairs wore clothing that worked well with the many khaki uniforms around them.

Award-winning costume designer Caroline McCall took over the costume department for seasons three and four, having previously assisted Susannah in season one. Even though it was her first major production, Caroline knew the cast and production team well. She was also familiar with the characters and their general color palettes, although by now the series had reached the Roaring Twenties and she knew she needed to bring some of the fashion forward, away from the Edwardian look. She also had two upstairs weddings to prepare for—Mary's and Edith's—not to mention the dressing of Cora's mother, Martha Levinson, played by Hollywood royalty Shirley MacLaine. "On taking the position, one of the first things I had to do was fly to the US to do fittings with Shirley!" says Caroline. As a result, she had little time to dwell on the challenges

that lay ahead, and would go on to win a BAFTA with Susannah Buxton for her work on season one, two Emmy nominations for her work on seasons three and four, and other awards.

By now *Downton Abbey* had become a major hit around the world, triggering a renewed interest in vintage fashion from the era, from beaded dresses to tweed suits, which ironically made it harder for the costume team to find original pieces that they could adapt for the show. Each season of *Downton Abbey* required around three hundred costumes, some of which were original garments that needed to be repaired and adapted for the cast. Others were made from scratch using contemporary or vintage fabrics and trims sourced from vintage shops and fairs. Many garments were also hired from specialist theatrical costumiers, principally Cosprop and Angels in London, who have had a long association with *Downton Abbey*. John Bright at Cosprop was of invaluable help to the costume team over the years, as were a number of talented artisans who provided their skills across many seasons: milliner Sean Barrett and jeweler Sophie Millard provided many of the hats and stunning items of jewelry and tiaras seen on screen, and bespoke tailor Chris Kerr made many of the men's suits for the later seasons and the films.

By the time season five came around, Anna Mary Scott Robbins, another costume designer who would go on to win awards and multiple nominations for her designs on the series, took over and remained at the helm for the final season and the subsequent two films. *Downton* was by far the biggest period production she had designed for at that time, and Anna relished the opportunity and the challenge presented by the then phenomenon of a series.

Here Anna explains in a bit more depth what went on behind the scenes in the preparation and shooting of the multi-episodic drama.

Edith and Cora are filmed taking a stroll. They hold parasols, which were still an essential accessory for ladies out during the day.

"By the time I took over the costume design, *Downton Abbey* had already become a global phenomenon, with the previous teams setting a high bar in terms of costume, and I felt the pressure of course. But I loved the show, so it was also very exciting and something of a game changer for me. I was completely new to the series, as was my team, and I imagined the process of taking it over to be a bit like a relay race: I wanted the handover to be as smooth and imperceptible as possible. The transition needed to be seamless for the audience because these well-known characters were fully developed and their story arcs were in motion. Plus, there was so much love for the series and huge ensemble cast that I knew I had no option but to get it right! I was tasked with bringing the characters fully into the decade, to embrace the epitome of what the 1920s represented from a fashion perspective, so it was a great point to join and be able to make my mark.

Like any designer, my preparation always begins with research. I immersed myself in the first four seasons and gathered thousands of images, a library of books, and other material from the period to get a sense of what was going on socially, culturally, and fashion-wise at the time. I've always loved the 1920s, so it was wonderful to be able to explore the era in real depth. And I built upon that research to develop the existing characters, balancing where they had come from with where they were headed, and where we might take them stylistically.

As soon as the scripts were made available to me—and on the series we would usually be issued them on a rolling basis—I'd read through them several times to get a sense of the stories and character arcs, flagging any big set pieces that might require more research. And from there I would create mood boards for each character or scene, referencing my earlier research and homing in on any specific inspiration, such as a Patou illustration for Lady Mary or a photograph from the time that evoked a certain sense of style for Lady Edith on a trip to London.

Early on, I'd meet with the director and producer to present these mood boards and discuss ideas, moving on to collaborate with the production designer and the hair and makeup designers. During prep, we would have tone meetings to bring the aesthetics of the various departments together. Filmmaking can be a wonderfully collaborative process, and on *Downton*, that collaboration was natural and easy, which built an early trust that the characters and their costumes were in safe hands.

At the very beginning of prep, I came on board for a short research period and was then joined by my supervisor, Michael Weldon, and assistant costume designer Kathryn Tart.

Michael was my right-hand person, heading up recruitment, looking after the schedule, and overseeing the budget and logistics during filming. Kathryn assisted me in terms of design and was critical in achieving the vision, helping to implement my ideas practically. We started scouring vintage shops and attending textile fairs together; shopping for original garments, trims, and fabrics; and building a wonderful network of vintage traders that I have gone on to work with for almost ten years now. Collectors of 1920s originals are as obsessive and passionate about the era as I am, and finding original, near-century-old gems is akin to treasure hunting. I love to use as many original pieces on a production as possible, to anchor the costumes in the period and to showcase the incredible fabrics and craftsmanship of a time, which, in some ways, can never be recreated, but especially not in a time-pressured costume workroom. We shopped in Paris, which is still very much a center for vintage as well as contemporary textiles, and in London and further afield, stockpiling beautiful silk, velvet, lace, lamé, and wools—or anything interesting that we might call upon further down the line.

The department would begin to increase when the workroom started a couple of months before filming. On the series, we had a cutter and three full-time makers who made, restored, and adapted hundreds of costumes across the series. We would start by "toiling" ideas and shapes (creating a toile, or prototype, of a costume in a mock cloth before making it in the final fabric) for fitting.

Our initial fitting with the cast would be two to three hours long, during which we would try on lots of pieces, originals or makes, assessing together what shapes worked and which didn't, looking at fabric and color suggestions, earmarking what might be great for a particular story day or moment in the script. (Scripts are broken down into scenes but also "story days"—that is, days within the fictional storyline where characters should be wearing the same costume during the day, carrying the same props, et cetera. There are usually four or five story days per episode.) The first fitting is a great guide for any costumes we might be missing and need to source or make. At the second fitting, I would then have put together potential lineups so we could discuss the costume journey as a whole alongside the character plots.

Story days can vary in length and time on screen; some are key and others a mere beat and they're over, so it's important to balance the focus of the story day with the importance of the scene for any particular character. If it's

a key moment for an individual character, I'll probably use the opportunity to introduce a new costume. If it is a day that will play out on screen in a dominant way, I'll look to introduce the strongest combination of looks for the most impact. It's always important to balance the introduction of new looks with re-wears so the way a character dresses day in, day out feels authentic. It's a constant balance between choosing costumes that are right for the character, scene, and setting and that feel believable within a working wardrobe.

About a month before filming, our crowd supervisor would come on board. This person oversees the costuming of the supporting cast and heads up the crowd department, which is quite a feat involving managing logistics, pulling and fitting costumes, and looking after the costumes on set.

As we neared shooting, the principal team would start with around a fortnight to set up the costume truck and then continue working throughout the shoot, managing and maintaining the costumes during filming and looking after the costumes on set and, by extension, the cast wearing them. The team is responsible for dressing the cast and overseeing the all-important continuity for each character. During filming, both the principal and crowd departments would increase significantly with the demands of the script, with big set pieces requiring many talented workers to help prep, set up, dress, and look after large numbers of costumes.

We were continually creating, prepping, and then establishing the costumes while beginning to design and construct costumes for the next block of new scripts as they came in. The shooting schedule was fast-paced and tightly programmed, so quite often once we were up and running, we worked in final fabrics from the beginning, which meant having to work quickly and accurately, frequently fitting on location only a day or so before the costume was required for filming. Our final fitting was typically in a pre-call before the cast member went to hair and makeup (HMU), with the costume establishing on camera a couple of hours after that. There were definitely a few last-minute alterations with all hands on deck on the costume truck, which made for some adrenaline-fueled early starts but also a huge sense of achievement once the actor stepped onto set looking fabulous.

I'd generally be on set to establish a new costume so I could set up the scene and check that the director and actor were happy. I would also instruct my costume standby on how the costume elements should be set and give notes on prep and maintenance—for example, how I'd like the necktie to be done, how I'd want the sash positioned, or whether the costume should be steamed or pressed—usually going in with the standby to dress the actor for the first time.

More often than not, we'd make final choices on jewelry on the same day, having laid out a short list of options and working with the actor to decide on the perfect piece. My team would give any hats or headpieces the final once-over before handing them over to HMU and work closely with the team to set them. My team were experts on costume protocol and the etiquette of the period and would have carefully plotted the hats, coats, and gloves from scene to scene in advance, looking to Alastair Bruce, our historical advisor, if any questions arose. The schedule would often have to work around the wearing of hats and their removal because of the impact on hair!

Downton Abbey was described as a juggernaut when I first came on board, and I definitely found that to be true. It's a very busy shoot and it can be highly pressurized, but that came with a great energy, with every department excelling, and with that common goal and experience carrying you along. I'm often asked what a typical day looks like for me during filming, and the honest answer is there is no typical day! But, as an example, I might start the day in my workroom reviewing what's been made the day before, handing over a new design, or perhaps doing a fitting. Next, I might travel into central London to source some fabric, then head to the set to establish a scene, before returning to the workroom to do a debriefing. In the evenings, with some peace and quiet at home, it was hard to switch off and not think about new designs or problem-solve something so I'd have an answer for my cutter the next morning. *Downton* was a job that I lived and breathed for nine months of each year I was on it.

Every department on *Downton Abbey* strove for the highest production value achievable, and when it came to the *Downton Abbey* films, the same was true. We all wanted to elevate it higher, push further. We were a close-knit team that shared a wonderful shorthand, and it felt like we all raised the bar to a truly cinematic level.

The films were different because instead of shooting multiple episodes over six months, we were shooting a single feature-length film over twelve weeks. I had a similar prep period for the films but welcomed a bigger costume team, this time with an additional assistant costume designer, a larger permanent crowd department, and an increased workroom with a cutter leading four to five makers. We also introduced a two-person dye room so we could dye fabric and break down costumes in-house.

From a costume point of view, *A New Era* required an even bigger team because there were almost twice as many story days and therefore more costumes and very diverse set pieces, including a wedding, a film set, village life, the French Riviera, and the funeral of the Dowager Countess, so there was a lot of ground to cover. I was asked to design *A New Era* in the summer of 2020, and I was expecting a baby that November, so knowing I'd be going back to work to prep the film when she was just weeks old, I decided to bring in additional design support. Maja Meschede came on board as my co–costume designer, and her creative talents were integral to the design process, which of course was made even more challenging with the COVID pandemic. We couldn't shop or source fabric in person, so the whole nature of our prep altered unrecognizably, and the logistics of fitting cast and operating as a team on and off set were complex. This all added an extra layer of difficulty to filming, especially with a fortnight shooting abroad. Despite this,

we all considered ourselves fortunate to be working and to be back together with a cast and crew more like a family than anything else. Both films have felt like wonderful reunions that I really cherish.

I'm totally passionate about what I do. I love storytelling through the medium of clothing, which provides a window into another era, so to bring those two elements together on a show with such a loyal worldwide audience has been a huge honor and privilege. This book celebrates some of the highlights of the series and the incredible stories behind many of the costumes and the evolving styles, and it has been a joy to be involved.

Below: Supporting artists are dressed and ready for filming. **Opposite:** (top) Anna Robbins on the set of the first *Downton Abbey* film; (bottom) Anna Robbins on set with Penelope Wilton (Isobel Grey).

ABOVE
STAIRS

ROBERT CRAWLEY

Earl of Grantham

Robert Crawley, seventh Earl of Grantham, was brought up an aristocrat, destined to inherit Downton Abbey from his father. He now co-owns the estate with his eldest daughter, Lady Mary, but he has always felt the weight of responsibility on him, that he must preserve Downton for future generations and play the part of an earl accordingly. To do this, he must conduct himself in the correct manner and dress appropriately, his wardrobe reflecting not just his elevated rank and age but also the season, occasion, and various social commitments expected of a lord.

For this reason, Robert must change clothing regularly throughout the day but with the minimum of fuss. Men, as Lady Gertrude Elizabeth Campbell put it in an etiquette manual of the era, were "supposed never to think about dress, nor talk about it." Robert might begin his day in tweeds if walking on the estate, then change into a morning suit for a church event. Later he might don some sporting attire for an afternoon's activity before changing into white tie for evening dinner. Valets were essential to the whole laborious process, and in Lord Grantham's case, it's Mr. Bates who helps him select his suits, cuff links, and correct tie for the events of the day.

All of Lord Grantham's suits would have been tailor-made in Savile Row, London, which was still the epicenter of bespoke tailoring in Britain. His clothing would have been made to last and cut from the finest fabric, Scottish tweeds, lined with silk for three-piece estate suits, and his bespoke shoes and boots made in the very best leather. Shirt collars were high, starched, and detachable, and Robert retains his stiff collars, although as the series progresses, the cravat tie and upright wing-tipped collar are gradually replaced by a more traditional tie and fold-down stiff collar. When we first meet Lord Grantham, a pocket watch is normally tucked into his waistcoat, but by the end of the series, he wears a wristwatch (as popularized by officers in the Great War who wore wristwatches in the trenches).

For filming, all of Lord Grantham's suits, as worn by Hugh Bonneville, were tailored for him. In establishing the look for Robert, Susannah Buxton, costume designer for the first season, ensured the tailoring of his clothing was suitable for the period and for the character of Robert: "Sharp shoulders, for example, would not have been right for the era, nor would they have suited Robert," explains Susannah. "I wanted a certain softness of coloring and tailoring to his suits. Robert is not a stiff, formal man. There is a gentleness to him, and I wanted him to look fairly relaxed."

Opposite: Lord Grantham wears a tailored three-piece tweed suit, with the bottom button of his waistcoat undone, a tradition made popular by King Edward VII.

The three-piece suit forms the mainstay of Lord Grantham's wardrobe, as was the case for most men in the early part of the twentieth century. For seasons five and six, Anna Robbins gradually introduced a number of new suits to reflect the slowly evolving changes, each designed to complement his existing wardrobe and to work within the backdrop of the rooms and estate of Downton Abbey. Robert wears this ginger suit for a number of daytime events, including at Brooklands to watch Mary's new beau, Henry Talbot, race his car.

A single-breasted, half Norfolk three-piece suit, the ginger herringbone tweed, with a faint windowpane (squared) check, is paired with a burgundy silk patterned tie and detachable Albany stiff collar. (The likes of Henry Talbot are commonly wearing soft collars, whereas Robert retains the traditional stiff collar.) Robert's look is accessorized with mother-of-pearl gold cuff links, and he accompanies the suit with chestnut brown stamped brogues (buffed and polished by Bates) and a brown felt homburg, a formal daytime hat popularized by Edward VII and increasingly favored in the 1920s.

The ginger herringbone tweed of Robert's suit, along with his burgundy tie, works well with the floral and pinks of Cora's flowered two-piece.

The years between 1912 and the late 1920s saw considerable changes to men's tailoring, as shown by the linen suit worn by Robert in season one and in the French Riviera some fifteen years later in *A New Era*. The four-button jacket gives way to three buttons, the lapel is deeper and wider on the later jacket, the upturned collar and cravat are replaced by a stiff, downturned collar and four-in-hand tie, there's a sharp crease down the middle of his trousers, and the pocket watch has gone.

For summery weather, a pale linen suit is still a must, but by the time Lord Grantham wears one in *A New Era*, the styling of his suits has moved on.

CORA CRAWLEY

The Countess of Grantham

The Countess of Grantham, Cora Crawley, has very much an Edwardian look when we first meet her at Downton Abbey. As befits her status and the era, she dresses sumptuously, her clothing of the highest quality, and her day wear includes blouses with high necks and skirts that touch the floor. Cora is still in a corset, although the fashionable silhouette in 1912 is a little softer and straighter than in earlier years.

As an American heiress, Cora has, since her marriage to Lord Grantham in 1890, had to adapt to the myriad of rules that govern aristocratic life in Britain. She is required to entertain influential guests, perform civic duties, and change her attire several times a day. By now she has mastered the art and always dresses elegantly and appropriately for every occasion. Her taste is classic, but she has an interest in fashion and its changing styles and is as cutting-edge as somebody of her generation could be. Like many American heiresses, she would have made a twice-yearly pilgrimage to Paris to attend fittings for clothing and to shop for the best accessories. Each season, she would have spent thousands on her clothing, and as a young married woman would have undoubtedly sourced much of her wardrobe from the House of Worth, a French fashion house that dressed many of Europe's and America's most influential and wealthy women.

As the years progress, Cora moves forward with fashion, but her signature look is very much imprinted in the first season, and certain elements remain throughout. She favors long, tailored jackets or coats and elegant, high-necked blouses, and her outfits and her clothing are often layered and draped. "There's a fluidity to many of the pieces that she wears," explains Anna Robbins. "She is always elegant and appropriate while demonstrating a flair for fashion in keeping with her American sensibilities."

Cora wears this sumptuous cream ensemble (opposite) in season one, when the Crawley family attend the village flower show. Susannah Buxton came across the dress and long jacket at the theatrical costumier Cosprop, which she then altered and finished to fit Elizabeth McGovern. She added some original black frogging (decorative braiding) as well, which gave real drama to the outfit. Susannah reworked a beautiful, wide-brimmed hat she also found at Cosprop, adding netting and various fabric adornments, to create an extravagant look for Cora.

Cora has an Edwardian look in season one and in the smaller image wears mauve, one of her signature colors. **Following spread:** The Countess of Grantham wears a skirt and jacket with an inbuilt cream satin waistcoat worn over a tulle blouse. It was remodeled from a found cream suit and retrimmed in black original trim. Her velvet coat features cream grosgrain fabric edging and is decorated with metallic cord and fabric flowers. The hat was restyled by Susannah and her team, and the outfit was worn in the garden party scene.

A good ten years later in the series, we see Cora in an eye-catching outfit that is illustrative of how far fashion has moved on—the corseted look has gone, the hemline has risen just a few inches above the ankle, and it has a simple, looser silhouette popular in the 1920s. The colors of this ensemble are particularly bold, with the terra-cotta silk of the coat contrasting with the teal-blue dress, which is an unusual look for the countess, who is more commonly seen in softer, more tonal colors of mauve, lilac, and cornflower blue.

The storyline dictated a more striking look for Cora—after feeling emotionally sidelined by Robert, she is flattered to receive attention from art historian Simon Bricker (played by Richard E. Grant). Under his admiring gaze, Cora blossoms and agrees to meet him at the National Gallery in London. Designer Anna Robbins purposely injected some bold colors into Cora's wardrobe to reflect the charged atmosphere of the scene but also to ensure that Cora stood out in the art gallery and as she walked with Bricker along the cobbled lamp-lit streets of London.

The original silk coat, which Anna found in Paris, has detailed knife-pleating panels and a scarf that attaches at the back, which Cora drapes around her neck. The teal dress was made by the workroom in contemporary morocain silk, although it is embellished by an original trim appliquéd down the center, front, and back. Cora also wore brown suede gloves—still a must when out and about in 1924—and a brown felt wide-brimmed hat.

Cora also wears her silk coat at a later event, a Remembrance Day ceremony in the village. Not every scene in *Downton Abbey* requires new clothing, and pieces are often worn more than once, just as in real life.

CHIFFON LAYERS

Cora wears this original 1920s evening dress in season six, when Mary's new admirer, Henry Talbot, comes for dinner. The chiffon layers are delicate and add movement, which is typical of Cora's style, and the dress is decorated with a silver bugle beading in a trailing floral design and chiffon flower detail on the hip.

At almost a century old, it's no surprise that the vintage dress required some restoration and customizing, both to restore some of its missing tambour beading and to ensure it draped well on Elizabeth McGovern. When it comes to beading, modern beads rarely match the size and patina of those of the 1920s, which meant that Anna Robbins and her team painstakingly sourced original beading from specialist vintage fairs. The shoulders were gathered and a chiffon insert was added to raise and soften the neckline to suit Cora, and a new slip was made to replace the perished one underneath and to add length to the gown.

The tiered chiffon layers and looser, straighter silhouette are a fashionable look for Cora, and the burgundy color suits her complexion.

In the first *Downton Abbey* movie, Cora wears an art deco–inspired blouse to greet the King and Queen on their arrival at the house. Elizabeth McGovern looks fantastic in long-line tunic blouses, and Anna Robbins was keen to design something that had real impact, yet wasn't too overwhelming for close-up shots. The blouse began life as an original embroidered silk tulle scarf that

Anna had come across: "It was six feet long and had a beautiful graphic design at both ends, embroidered with minute chain stitch in metallic thread. I wanted to use both ends for the front and back of a blouse, and it was a complex pattern-cutting feat to ensure the various motifs sat in the right place and in a proportionally flattering manner. Every edge and motif was used in some way, be it as part of the collar or cuffs."

The positioning of the trim is planned and perfected on the stand before being made into a striking blouse for Cora.

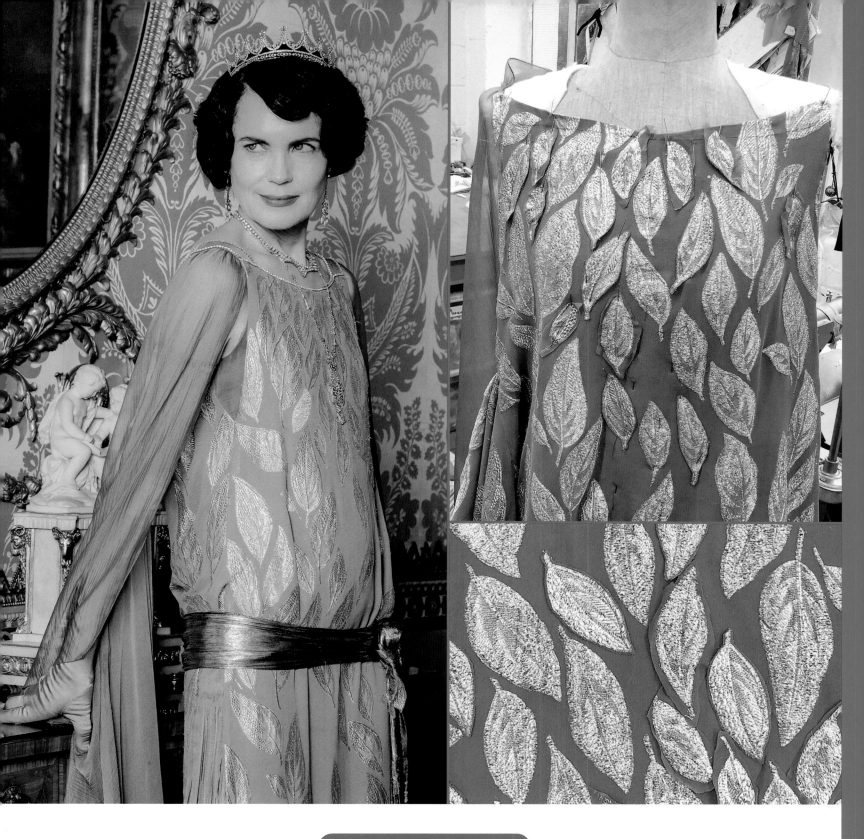

GLITTERING BALL

The first movie also features a spectacular ball with the royal family, to which Cora wears a silk chiffon tabard gown with a cowled back and sheer, draped chiffon sleeves that fall from her shoulders to the floor. The dress began life as a length of turquoise silk with silver-leaf lamé, which was originally earmarked for Edith because its beautiful turquoise color was a real signature hue for her. In the end, the royal ball provided an opportunity to use the fabric for Cora, but only after Anna Robbins had checked that it could be dyed a soft mauve, as the turquoise color would not have been right for Cora. Anna's team also hand cut some of the leaves, appliquéing them back onto the chiffon to achieve an ombré effect, with denser coverage on the bodice and bottom of the train. The gown was finished with diamanté trim and an original length of silver lamé worked into a sash worn low on Cora's hips.

The dress Cora wore to the royal ball was designed first on paper (opposite) and then on a stand before it finally appeared on camera.

MARTHA LEVINSON

Cora's mother, Martha Levinson, makes a dramatic statement when she first arrives at Downton Abbey for Mary's wedding to Matthew. Dressed in a fur-trimmed coat and matching plumed hat, she cuts a striking figure, a confident and wealthy American who clearly embraces new fashions. In many ways, she is the opposite of Violet: She is forward-thinking, happy to talk about money (which Violet deems vulgar), and more flamboyant and showier in appearance than Violet.

Costume designer Caroline McCall had a fabulous time dressing Shirley MacLaine, the Academy Award–winning Hollywood star who played Martha. At the end of season four, Martha arrives with Cora's brother Harold, for Lady Rose's debutante season. Martha needed to wear an outfit that had real impact, which Caroline achieved by dressing her in a terracotta embroidered silk coat and hat that beautifully matched Martha's auburn hair. The coat was made by Claire Ramsell, with feather-trimmed cuffs and hem inspired by a period photo Caroline found of a French society woman. Martha wears this over an original devoré tabard dress, which was altered and dyed by the costume team, along with a straw brimmed hat adorned with pheasant feathers, silk motifs, and a vintage bird-of-paradise plume.

Violet and Martha dress very differently. Violet keeps to the Edwardian fashion of lace-trimmed, high-necked outfits, whereas Martha looks far more modern and glamorous in a luxurious fur-trimmed coat and turban adorned with large feather plumes.

GARDEN PARTIES AND AFTERNOON TEA

The Crawley family, like all members of the aristocracy, make a careful selection of their outfits according to the occasion and time of day. As Lady Gertrude Elizabeth Campbell put it in her *Etiquette of Good Society*, "A dress which would look perfectly well on one occasion will appear out of place and vulgar on another," and this complex set of rules governed Edwardian life. Morning attire was simple, refined, and a little more practical, whereas dresses at an afternoon garden party or bazaar could be a little brighter and prettier, with the young "in delicately tinted fine materials . . . [and the elder ladies wearing] silks or some handsome material, richly trimmed with lace, a foreign shawl or lace mantle."

Those expectations of dress are very much in evidence in *Downton Abbey*. We see members of the household at a variety of daytime events, which include paying calls on neighbors (often the homes of Violet or Isobel) or attending garden parties and fêtes in the village, where they are very much in the public eye. In the first season, the Crawley family make an appearance at the village flower show, and in the final episode, the Crawleys hold a garden party on the lawn of Downton, where the guests mill around the marquees looking elegant in their summer afternoon outfits, their garments awash with lace trimmings, delicate and gauzy materials, and straw hats. During the party, Robert, dressed in a cream linen suit, stiff collar, and cravat, receives a telegram and announces to their guests that war has broken out with Germany.

This scene was deliberately stylized by Susannah Buxton with everyone wearing cream or black and white for dramatic effect. Edith wore a dress previously worn in the Merchant Ivory Productions' *A Room with a View* and remodeled to fit her. Mary's dress was a make in striped cotton used in reverse with an original lace collar, and Sybil wore a bought cotton dress from about 1912. The servants of the household are dressed in their formal uniforms—the footmen and Carson in white tie and the maids in their frilly aprons and black dresses—clothing that is normally reserved for the evening or whenever the family is entertaining.

Following spread: The Crawley family attend the village flower show wearing soft cream linens and cottons with lace gloves and wide-brimmed straw hats. The downstairs staff wear their Sunday best in soft grays and blues.

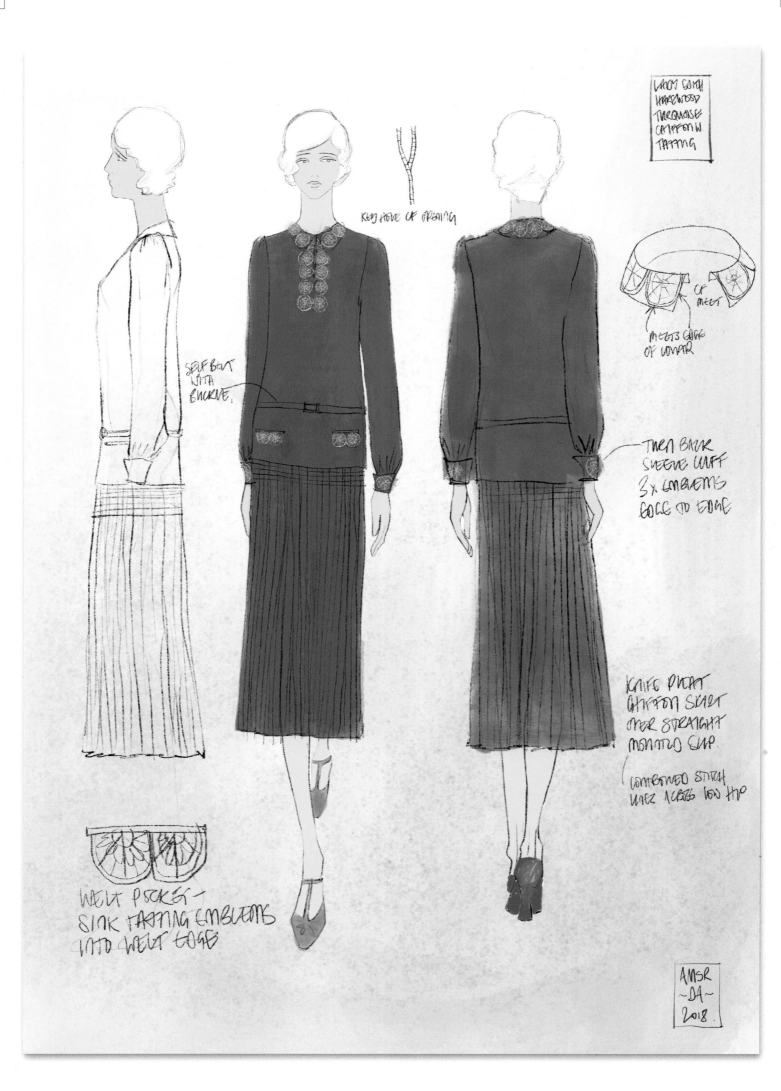

LADY EDITH
HAREWOOD
TURQUOISE
CHIFFON W.
TATTING

KEY HOLE OF OPENING

SELF BELT
WITH
BUCKLE.

CF MEET

MEETS EDGE
OF COLLAR

TURN BACK
SLEEVE CUFF
3x EMBLEMS
GOES TO EDGE

WELT POCKETS -
SILK TATTING EMBLEMS
INTO WELT EDGE

KNIFE PLEAT
CHIFFON SKIRT
OVER STRAIGHT
MOUNTED SLIP.

CONTRASTING STITCH
LINE ACROSS LOW HIP

AMSR
~DA~
2018.

In the first *Downton Abbey* movie, Edith, Cora, and Mary are invited to call on Princess Mary, daughter of King George and Queen Mary. As a result, they must wear clothing that is suitable for afternoon tea but also formal enough for a royal visit. Anna Robbins's challenge was to achieve that balance while also creating outfits, including hats and coats, that worked well across the trio.

Edith wears a sea-green silk georgette dress that was inspired by an original two-piece made up of a belted tunic over a mounted pleated skirt. "We hand appliquéd tatting motifs [intricate hand lacework] onto the tunic," explains Anna, "having dyed them three different colors to give an ombré effect. The coat was also a contemporary make, and its lovely sea-green color worked with the dress and hat. I loved how it all came together, and this is one of my favorite looks for Edith.

"Cora's outfit is made up of a layered tunic of lace and pleated silk to create a really elegant look. We paired the dress with an original and unusual chartreuse wool coat, sourced from the Parisian hire house Aram, which has incredible decorative tape work and looks stunning on Cora."

Mary looks particularly striking in a printed silk dress that has an interesting story behind it. "I found a dress with a lovely printed silk as part of it at a vintage fair in London," reveals Anna. "It was filled with hedgerows and fields, a church, and a village, and I thought, that's the Downton estate! But the dress itself was oversized and damaged. We salvaged as much of the silk as we could and then sent it off to a digital printing company to replicate the print onto new fabric so we had enough to do a new make.

"We created the body out of the new silk, but the sleeves and waterfall drapes are from the original lighter-weight fabric, all bound off in navy to give it a graphic edge that suited Lady Mary down to the ground. I loved the blue of her hat with feather trim, and we made her cashmere coat, which was inspired by a Paul Poiret design, using an original trim dyed to match."

Anna Robbins created elegant and interesting looks for Edith, Cora, and Mary, which are perfect for afternoon tea with a princess.

LADY MARY
HAREWOOD
'ESTATE'
PRINT DRESS

STAND COLLAR
W/ HIDDEN
PLACKET

SLEEVE &
WAISTBAND
DRAPE IN
ORIGINAL SILK

DROPPED WAISTBAND

NAVY SILK
BONDED EDGE

AMSR
~DA~
2018.

HATS AND GLOVES

Downton Abbey features a vast array of hats and gloves, as they were deemed essential items of wear right up to the Second World War and beyond. Everyone from Lord Grantham to Daisy, the kitchen maid, wears a hat when they're out in public, and a myriad of rules governed when hats or gloves could be removed. Men could take off their hats when entering a building or church, or as a mark of respect when talking to someone, or they might doff their hat to a lady as they walked by. Women usually kept their hats on anywhere outside the home, partly because it was a laborious process pulling out hairpins and re-dressing hair (especially without a lady's maid).

The Edwardian era saw something of a craze for large, flamboyant hats on women, and in the early seasons, we see a plethora of large-brimmed creations adorned with exotic feathers, silk flowers, ribbons, tulle, and other embellishments. Lighter straw hats were worn in summer, velvet or felt hats in winter, all perched on top of elaborate hairstyles and secured with an array of hatpins.

The brimless toque, a favorite of the Dowager Countess, had also become common during the Edwardian era, thanks partly to Queen Mary, who was frequently seen in one. A variety of other hat styles emerged, such as the military-influenced bicorne hat that Cora wears during the wartime years. Thereafter, oriental-style turbans, decorated headdresses, and bandeaux (headbands) worn low on the forehead and sometimes adorned with jewelry or feathers—a popular 1920s flapper look—were prevalent, although wide-brimmed hats retained their appeal throughout the decade.

Opposite: In season two, Cora looks striking in a bicorne hat, an upturned-brim style briefly popular during the First World War. **Below:** The many different types of hats worn by the ladies of Downton Abbey, all of them adorned with feathers, embroidery, fabric flowers, or pom-poms. **Following spread:** Lady Mary's wedding to Henry Talbot saw a variety of stunning hats on display.

THE CLOCHE

As the 1920s progress, we see the ladies increasingly wearing cloches, bell-shaped hats (the French word *cloche* means "bell") that were often pulled down low over the forehead. Usually made of felt or straw, they acted as the perfect frame for the fashionable cropped bob hairstyle. Here, Mary and Edith wear cloches in different styles. Inspired by a fashion illustration of the time, Mary's, with its fanned ribbon work, has quite an edgy, graphic look and is perfect for her. Edith's cloche, which is adorned with a blue flower and has an asymmetrical upturned brim, was created by milliner Sean Barrett, who has had a long association with *Downton Abbey*.

Anna Robbins also worked closely with Sean, as she describes: "Sean has an incredible workshop, full of vintage trims and hat blocks, and he's a real source of inspiration when it comes to period millinery. I would typically go to Sean with my research and ideas, usually with first-fitting photos and fabric swatches and with an idea of the general shape and proportions of the hat I was after. We'd discuss ideas, and it was always such a fun, collaborative process. Often Sean would become animated about some embroidered turn-of-the-century silk trim stashed away in his attic, and he'd come back with armfuls of spectacular vintage trims. I'd procrastinate for a while because it was so difficult to decide which trim was more beautiful, and he'd then get to work. Sean's hats are beautiful, and Violet's in particular were always sensational, and they were invariably fun to do."

The younger members of the Downton household wear fashionable cloche hats, while Isobel and Violet retain their brimmed versions.

GLOVES

Etiquette demanded that the ladies of *Downton Abbey* wear gloves in every season and around the clock: delicate crochet for summer days, along with long gloves in the evening, kid leather giving way almost exclusively to silk gloves in the later series of *Downton*. Under the watchful eye of historical advisor Alastair Bruce, the costume and production team had to be mindful of the complex rules surrounding the wearing of gloves. A lady could keep her gloves on when drinking tea or a glass of Champagne, but she would be expected to take them off to eat, and for dinner they were removed once seated. She could place them on her lap to be covered by a napkin, but they should be back on after dinner, preferably discreetly done under the table. Even in the 1920s, when there was a certain relaxation of dress codes for women, gloves were still deemed an important item of wear and a fashionable accessory.

In high society, a lady never entertained or went out without her gloves, and even in the 1920s, it was still deemed risqué not to wear a pair.

Men's hats were a wardrobe staple of the 1920s and were both fashionable and functional, signifying status and wealth but also protecting the wearer from the elements. They were worn outside and at sporting events and within certain public spaces, such as hotels or office lobbies. Inside, however, hats were normally taken off, especially when visiting a person's home, in contrast to the ladies, who kept their hats on when paying a visit. Hats were removed to eat, when greeting someone, and as a mark of respect.

Men's hats changed according to the seasons, as they did for women, with felts and wools favored in the cooler months and straw often worn in the summer. We see the men in *Downton Abbey* wearing a variety of styles. Lord Grantham has many in his wardrobe, from military peaked caps and silk top hats worn to weddings and formal engagements to civilian homburgs, flat caps, and panamas worn in the village, on the estate, and on holiday in the Mediterranean, respectively. Homburgs were a staple for the professional middle and upper classes, having developed from the bowler, and this is the hat Matthew Crawley is wearing when we first meet him. Working men would probably own just one flat cap, made from wool or tweed. Thomas wears one in season one, but then dons a homburg and a bowler as he rises through the ranks below stairs. Mr. Carson and Mr. Bates also wear bowlers, which befit a butler and a valet.

A variety of hats are worn by the men of *Downton Abbey*. (From top left, top to bottom) We see Tom in a felt trilby, Mr. Bates in a straw fedora, Thomas in a bowler, Sir Anthony Strallan doffing a top hat, Lord Merton in a fedora, and Lord Grantham in a wool six-panel cap as part of his estate wear.

VIOLET CRAWLEY

The Dowager Countess

Violet, the Dowager Countess, is a firm believer in the rules of social hierarchy, in which etiquette and the correct forms of dress play a vital part. Born in 1842, Violet grew up in a world in which white tie and tails and tiaras at dinner were the norm. The aristocracy was morally obliged to behave and dress impeccably, and its members knew their place and understood the rules. Violet is thus aghast when she witnesses the gradual erosion of the rules, and some of her best quips are reserved for those who contravene them: When Robert wears a tuxedo for dinner, she suggests he might next come down in pajamas or his dressing gown. As *Downton*'s creator, Julian Fellowes, puts it, "Violet hates black tie because she regards it as a sign that everything is falling apart. And, of course, one of the reasons the old system came to an end is that great swathes of the upper class didn't want to play anymore. They didn't want to have their lives dominated by when luncheon had to be served and the rest of it."

With her own wardrobe, Violet remains firmly wedded to an Edwardian style of dress with high necklines, floor-length skirts, and a corseted look. She is a fan of the large plumed hat, which often serves to accentuate her presence or mood, as does the cane she resolutely grasps. Season one costume designer Susannah Buxton looked to the real-life figures of Queen Alexandra and Queen Mary to provide inspiration for Violet's style. As consorts to King Edward VII and George V, respectively, they would have been contemporaries of Violet and were trendsetters for aristocratic women of the time. Their strong silhouettes, which both queens retained throughout their lives, also suited Violet's dominant character. Queen Mary, in particular, favored tailored ensembles in dusky pastels as well as crown-like toque hats, often with an umbrella or cane in her hand, just as Violet does.

When it came to Violet's palette, Susannah initially dressed the dowager in stronger colors than the usual pastel shades favored by Edwardian ladies—blacks, purples, and greens—to reflect Violet's overbearing nature. Later in the series and in the movies, Violet's palette softens, and we see her in faded blues, greens, and grays, but her hems stay firmly floor-length and her necklines high, her style still closer to the turn of the century than to the Roaring Twenties.

Violet's look was partly based on the Edwardian style icons Queen Alexandra (left) and Queen Mary (right, with George V).

Early on in season one, Isobel and Matthew Crawley come to Downton Abbey for dinner, where they are introduced to the whole of the Crawley family for the first time. They line up in their evening splendor, and Violet looks every inch the grandee, dressed in a sumptuous black silk dress, her jet necklace and choker glinting in the candlelight. She is an imposing sight, and when Isobel asks in an informal manner what they should call each other, Violet can't help but give a typically withering reply: "Well, we could always start with Mrs. Crawley and Lady Grantham."

The dress, made up of a jet beaded bodice, "leg of mutton" sleeves, and a belted silk jacquard bustled skirt, conforms to Violet's signature style. The bodice is worn over a tulle infill, and the whole outfit was made by the costume department from scratch using original trims and contemporary fabric, and then hand embroidered with jet beads and sequins. Violet's costumes were often multilayered and richly detailed and frequently took the costume team many hours to craft.

Opposite and below: In season one, Violet wears this teal-green two-piece dress with an embroidered, belted waistcoat and heavily decorated black tulle infill. Her taffeta silk ruched toque was made by the costumier Cosprop using fragments of original fabric and trimmings.

As the series progresses, we see Violet in softer colors: mauves rather than strong purple and soft blues rather than emerald greens. While Violet's silhouette remains largely the same, the detailing, textures, and fabrics for her garments gradually evolve to reflect the 1920s—the style of fabrics available change with the times and so too must the bespoke creations. It's a subtle shift, and yet there are still nods to the overarching trends of the time. In the first movie, Violet wears a mauve dress to greet the King and Queen when they arrive at Downton Abbey. The dress started life as a large ivory Chinese embroidered shawl from the period, which Anna Robbins dyed along with the accompanying trims and textiles. The asymmetrical brim of her hat, embellished with satin ribbon, beading, and a flank of vintage bird-of-paradise, adds a certain flair to the outfit.

Violet and the rest of the household wait on the drive outside Downton, ready to greet the King and Queen.

VIOLET AND ISOBEL

Violet and Isobel are something of a double act in *Downton Abbey*. With very different perspectives on life, they initially disagree about most matters and had some delightful spats. Violet eventually softens toward Isobel, perhaps because the latter refused to be worn down by the dowager's snobbery, and the two became trusted friends.

As a result, the pair often appear in scenes together wearing complementary outfits balancing palette and tone while maintaining their individual styles. At Mary's wedding in season six, Violet's cream ensemble complements Isobel's light blue suit, and in season five they both look striking as they take tea in the garden, with Isobel in a rich blue and Violet in a pale sage green.

By season six, Isobel and Violet are firm friends, and they both look stylish in their own way at the wedding of Lady Mary and Henry.

Violet wears an original Edwardian walking suit in both the first and second movies. It consists of a long jacket and skirt in cream linen, decorated with intricate lace insertion, tape work, and hand embroidery. Maggie Smith was delighted by the find, marveling at the craftsmanship of the piece. In the first movie, she wears it with a hat with an asymmetric swept brim decorated with an aigrette of vintage osprey, and in the second film without a hat, as she watches the making of a silent movie in the house.

The Dowager Countess looks resplendent in an original cream linen walking suit, which can be seen in both *Downton* films.

"The metallic gold lace on Violet's dress was discovered at Portobello Market, unused and in its original paper packaging. I used the lace on the bodice and skirts as well as the layered sleeve Violet typically wears, which provided coverage of her arm to the elbow while also working with a glove."

—ANNA ROBBINS

EVENING FINERY

When Carson rings the gong for dinner, we see the characters of *Downton Abbey* dressed in their full splendor. For the women, day wear is replaced by ornate evening dress, even if it's just the family dining, with long silk or kid gloves and jewels and tiaras that sparkle in the evening light. The men change out of their daytime attire into formal white tie.

Evening dresses are made of sumptuous fabrics, often exquisitely beaded. Even more elaborate attire is required for balls or when entertaining noble or royal guests. Strict codes of dress surround these events, and Edwardian high society delighted in ridiculing anyone who dressed incorrectly. The real-life Duchess of Marlborough and American heiress Consuelo Vanderbilt Balsan often marveled at the observance of ritual in the Edwardian era. "I can remember a dinner in honor of the Prince and Princess of Wales at which I wore a diamond crescent instead of the prescribed tiara. The Prince with a severe glance at my crescent observed, 'The Princess has taken the trouble to wear a tiara. Why have you not done so?' Luckily, I could truthfully answer that I had been delayed by some charitable function in the country and that I had found the bank in which I kept my tiara closed on my arrival in London."

As we move into the 1920s, evening wear is still formal but reflects the changing fashions: Hemlines gradually rise and waistlines drop, and we see exotic embroidery, beadwork, and tassels, and jeweled or feathered headbands. By the mid- to late 1920s, the Jazz Age is in full swing, and dresses have a straighter, looser silhouette, with undulating hemlines in lamés, glossy silks, and glittering sequins. There is a play on layered skirts and fringed edges to accentuate movement, harnessing the energy of the period and its musical influences. Fashions are more risqué in London and the cities, where the likes of Edith, Rose, and Mary can head out to restaurants and clubs no longer under the watchful eye of the family. Back at Downton Abbey, evening dress is a little more pared back and restrained, and it will be some time yet before the family and their guests stop dressing for dinner.

Opposite: Mary appears with Henry at the Criterion restaurant in London wearing a green silk bias-cut dress overlaid with metallic embroidery. Her bare shoulders and gold lamé headband make for a quintessential 1920s look.

White tie was once the only acceptable attire for evening wear at Downton, consisting of a tailcoat, formal trousers, white waistcoat, starched white shirt, and white bow tie. As dress codes relaxed, however, black tie became more prevalent in the evening, much to the horror of the Dowager Countess, who mistakes Robert for a waiter when a wardrobe mix-up downstairs requires him to don a black dinner jacket and tie.

Nonetheless, as the pendulum swings toward the informality of black tie, we still see white tie at Downton, worn particularly when the Crawleys entertain high-ranking guests. The suiting featured at right was made by Anna Robbins's go-to tailor, Chris Kerr, using traditional tailoring techniques mirroring tailoring from the mid-1920s but fitted to the modern frame (in this case, Robert Crawley and Henry Talbot).

White tie consists of a wool cutaway tailcoat typically in barathea with black silk–faced lapels, worn open and cut away to form points just below the waist, and tails falling to the back of the knees. It is paired with formal trousers, a white, low-cut starched waistcoat, a starched bib-fronted shirt with detachable wing-tipped collar, and a white bow tie, and is accessorized with mother-of-pearl dress studs and gold cuff links.

Black tie is made up of a single-breasted, wool three-piece tuxedo or dinner-jacket suit worn with a white starched shirt with detachable wing-tipped collar and a black silk bow tie, onyx dress studs, and gold cuff links. The word *tuxedo* originated in America in the late 1880s, named after Tuxedo Park, a gated community in upstate New York and the site of a country club where the formal wear was first worn.

Lord Grantham wears traditional white tie for evening dinner, while Henry Talbot dresses in black tie, which was increasingly favored by younger gentlemen.

I n season six, we see some of the family gather for dinner at Rosamund's London house. The mood is somber, as they've spent the day at Brooklands racing circuit, where one of Henry Talbot's fellow racers lost his life in a crash. The men are in black tie—even Robert, who, at Downton Abbey, would normally be seen in white tie—and the women look stylish in their evening wear, both Edith and Mary wearing beaded, jeweled headbands.

Despite the day's earlier tragedy, Edith and Bertie have something to be happy about, as it's later that evening that Bertie proposes to Edith, confessing that he's mad about her, with Edith sweetly answering, "I don't ever think I'm the sort of girl men are mad about." She wears a delicate, original 1920s dress in lemon sorbet that Anna Robbins sourced from a London vintage fair. "I picked this dress because the tones worked in such harmony with the soft lighting and setting, so the whole moment felt romantic and golden," explains Anna. "It was beautifully decorated with seed beading, sequins, and embroidery. We had to carefully restore it and add a chiffon layer with mirrored scallop hem to bring the dress to just below the knee, something we often have to do with our leading ladies, as they are tall."

Edith's dress is an original 1920s piece, its delicate seed pearl beading and sequins glinting beautifully in the soft evening light.

Only the very best formal attire will do when holding a ball, especially if that ball is held in honor of the King and Queen, as was the case in the first *Downton Abbey* film. Etiquette dictated the most formal style of evening dress for the gents, reserved for regal occasions, which consisted of white tie and tailcoat worn with black breeches, black silk stockings, and patent buckled pumps. The women wore formal evening gowns accessorized with their finest tiaras and jewelry, pulling out all the stops for their eminent guests.

Mary and Violet were dressed in beautifully decorative evening dresses designed by Anna Robbins to work together, aspects of their form faintly mirroring each other with others in stark contrast. Mary, representing the future of Downton Abbey, is dressed in striking high contrast swirling black-and-silver beading. Violet, representing the abbey's past, is dressed in palest blue with soft, silver embroideries, her palette muted and almost ghostly—beautiful and ornate and still regal in stature but a fading version of a once imperious character.

Opposite: Anna Robbins: "I think this is my favorite costume for Violet. I found some exquisite original silk embroidered tulle at Portobello Market that I knew would be perfect for her. The tulle formed the sleeves and infill, and we appliquéd the embroidery to the layered silk skirts, finally adding antique beaded fringing and tassels rescued from a beautiful but perished couture gown." **Following spread:** Anna Robbins crafted Mary's dress out of an original she obtained from a specialist vintage trader that was much shorter and with a higher neckline. "The beading was astonishing," Anna says. "I'd never found anything like this before. I wanted to make the dress floor-length, so we painstakingly mapped out the bead placement and continued the beading down the extended length. We altered the neckline and added long velvet drapes from the shoulders. When she's waltzing around the dance floor, it flows beautifully."

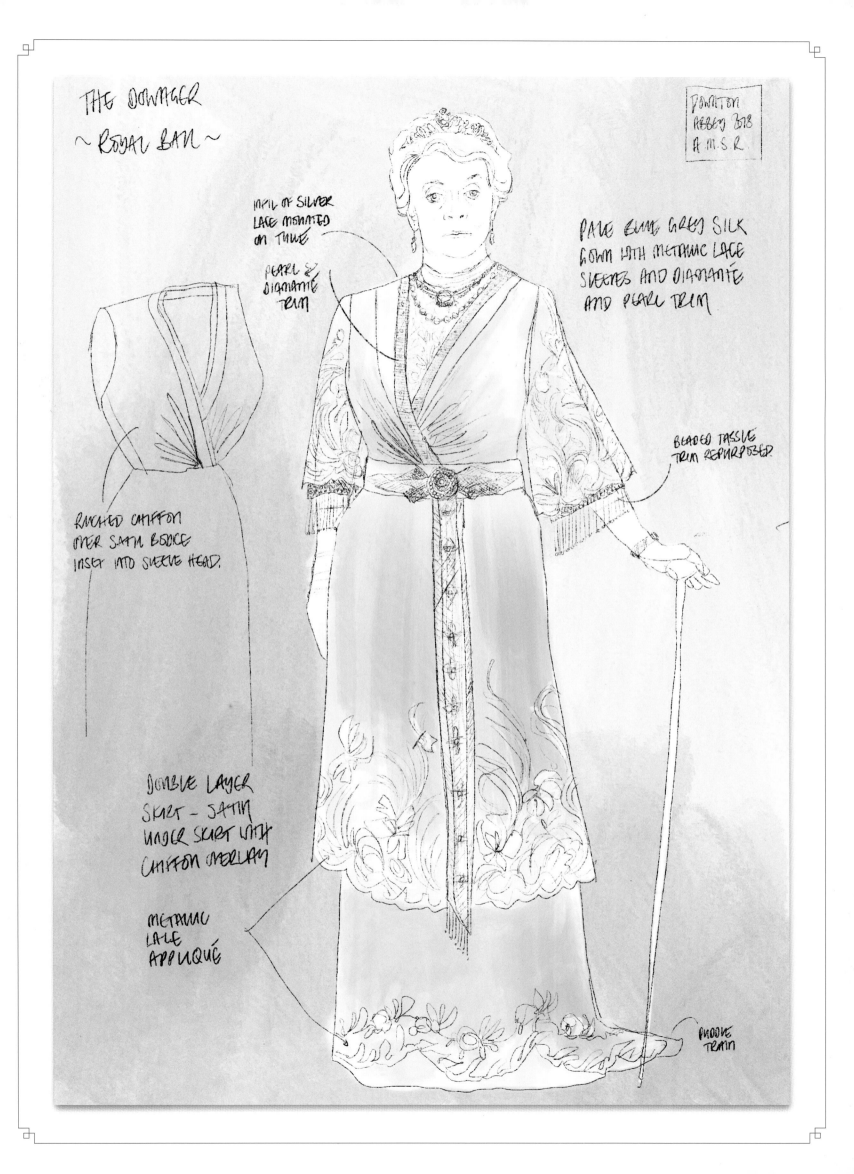

THE DOWAGER
~ ROYAL BALL ~

DOWNTON
ABBEY 2018
A.M.S.R

INFIL OF SILVER
LACE MOUNTED
ON TULLE

PEARL &
DIAMANTÉ
TRIM

PALE BLUE GREY SILK
GOWN WITH METALLIC LACE
SLEEVES AND DIAMANTÉ
AND PEARL TRIM

RUCHED CHIFFON
OVER SATIN BODICE
INSET INTO SLEEVE HEAD.

BEADED TASSLE
TRIM REPURPOSED

DOUBLE LAYER
SKIRT - SATIN
UNDER SKIRT WITH
CHIFFON OVERLAY

METALLIC
LACE
APPLIQUÉ

PUDDLE
TRAIN

No evening outfit was complete without jewelry and adornments for the hair. Aristocrats like the Crawleys could afford to wear precious gemstones, some of which were family heirlooms or were given as part of a wedding trousseau. While only married women could wear tiaras for white-tie engagements, single ladies instead wore decorative hair adornments with feathers, silk scarves, and jeweled headpieces worn low on the forehead, which was de rigueur in the 1920s.

Jewelry is an important part of the costume department's responsibility and is often the finishing touch to a look. It can be hired, from costumiers Cosprop and Angels or specialist jeweler Sophie Millard, or sourced by the design team. "It's hard not to collect vintage jewelry when I find it. Special pieces tend to jump out as perfect for a particular character, and I'll squirrel them away for an opportune moment," says Anna Robbins. "I also loved working with Sophie Millard, who has a huge stock of inspiring period jewelry spanning the centuries. With an idea, a sketch, or a swatch of the dress fabric, she would offer us a perfect set of accessories to match, either original pieces or a bespoke customization of vintage parts. Sophie Millard supplied jewelry for most of our principal women as well as the dress studs, cuff links, and watches for the gents, and the attention to detail within the huge volume of jewelry supplied for our supporting cast was staggering."

The costume department works closely with the hair and makeup team, as adornments need to work with hair styles and hair needs to be designed around hair accessories and tiaras.

Decorative hairpins (bottom right) and headpieces worn low on the forehead were a fashionable look in the 1920s, which Rose combines with preserved flowers in her hair for her wedding.

S ome very special items of jewelry have been loaned to the makers of *Downton Abbey*. Bentley & Skinner, jewelers by royal appointment, loaned tiaras across the series and both films, including the tiara worn by Lady Mary for her wedding, tiaras worn by Violet, Cora, and Lady Edith at the royal ball, and Lucy's wedding jewelry. "The jewelry for the royal ball was worth an eye-watering sum of money and was kept in a safe when not on set," says Anna Robbins, with Violet's Victorian tiara totaling 16.5 carats of brilliant-cut diamonds and Cora's Edwardian headpiece consisting of 8 carats.

Anna Robbins also worked with model maker Martin Adams to replicate some well-known royal jewels for the King, Queen, and Princess Mary in the first *Downton* film. A copy of the Order of the Garter for the King, the Vladimir Tiara and Cambridge Emeralds parure for Queen Mary, and Princess Mary's Fringe Tiara were all faithfully reproduced.

LADY MARY
TALBOT

Over the years, Lady Mary's look has evolved to reflect her changed circumstances and the rapidly changing world in which she lives, but she has always had a signature style. She is elegant and projects a classic simplicity, and her tall, slender figure and dark hair, which she later cuts into a shingle bob, perfectly suit the evolving fashions and silhouette of the 1920s.

The eldest daughter to Robert and Cora, Mary is a young girl when we first meet her, inexperienced in the ways of the world, but mindful of her duty to the Downton Abbey estate and intent upon marrying well. There is a ruthlessness to her, as her heart has not yet softened as it does in later years, and she is initially prepared to marry the heir to the estate, Patrick Crawley, whom she clearly never loved and little mourned when he died on the *Titanic*.

Mary, along with her two younger sisters, must perform the usual duties expected of a titled family—dressing for dinner, attending flower shows and garden parties—and it's perhaps to while away the tedium of her days that she delights in goading her younger sister Edith. It's no wonder also that she's drawn to hunting or to attractive male visitors (with disastrous consequences in season one) in an otherwise staid existence. As she puts it to Matthew Crawley: "Women like me don't have a life. We choose clothes and pay calls and work for charity and do the season, but really we're stuck in a waiting room until we marry."

Mary's public duties extend to attending the village flower show with her family, and here she wears a cotton summer dress in mauve and ivory stripes, which she also dons later in the season at a garden party at Downton. By now, dresses have moved away from the S-bend silhouette common at the turn of the century to a straighter, more natural line. The costumier Cosprop made this dress using contemporary striped cotton sourced from Shepherd's Bush Market in London, but reversed to fade the colors. An original lace collar and silk belt was added and Mary also wears a wide-brimmed straw hat and pearls. Susannah Buxton based many of Mary's garments on a collection of clothes owned by the Edwardian socialite Heather Firbank. "She was a fashionable woman of her time without being fussy."

Heather Firbank and her fine collection of clothes, now housed in the Victoria and Albert Museum in London, provided the inspiration for many of Lady Mary's costumes in the early series of *Downton Abbey*.

Mary wears this black lace tiered evening gown in season two, first at the regimental dinner held at Downton Abbey, and then at a couple of other evening events later in the season. It goes well with the scarlet mess uniforms around her, and the scooped neck looks pretty against her pale skin. It's something of a go-to evening dress for Mary during this wartime period, when the ladies of the household were still dressing sumptuously but not updating their outfits as often as they once did or dressing in an overtly flamboyant manner.

Susannah Buxton knew as soon as she spotted the unusual velvet-ribboned sleeves at a London market that they would work well on a dress for Mary. She and her team made the dress to go with the sleeves, using lace from a train belonging to a vintage dress over a smoky blue chiffon layer. The bodice fits snugly over a corset, which Mary is still wearing in this period, and she also wears a long strand of jet beads.

The dark color of Lady Mary's understated but pretty lace evening gown complements Matthew's scarlet mess uniform.

MARRIAGE PROPOSAL

Mary often wears strong colors, such as deep burgundies and navy blues, which reflect her direct and resolute nature while also complementing her complexion. This now iconic dress in deep burgundy was worn by Mary when Matthew Crawley finally proposed to her after a long will-they-or-won't-they romance. In falling for Matthew, Mary softens, and she is not quite the hard-edged girl she once was.

The tiered dress, which was made in-house, was based on an original scalloped-bottomed dress of the period. "I didn't want the dress to overshadow the scene," says Susannah Buxton, "so I designed something that was quite simple and dramatic. I knew also that she would be dancing outside on a snowy night and it needed to pick up light, so we chose silk taffeta." The shape for the dress was made in toile first—silk taffeta is an expensive fabric, so it was best to cut the taffeta after a few fittings. The tiered scalloped edging was also hand beaded, and a vintage flat diamanté buckle was sewn onto the neckline for added detail. Mary wears the dress with black evening gloves.

Lady Mary's silk taffeta dress perfectly suited the snowy setting and the romance of Matthew's marriage proposal.

Lady Mary becomes increasingly involved in the running of the Downton estate, and in doing so, we see her in various types of workwear and her version of a three-piece tweed suit. As Anna Robbins puts it, "This more androgynous look tapped into an emerging trend for women in the 1920s, but it also shows Mary in a different light, as she embarks on her career as a strong woman working in a man's world." The neat, tailored suit worn often with a tie mirrored the leaner, more linear silhouette of the 1920s, and Mary absolutely nails the look.

The three-piece double-breasted wool suit is a bespoke in-house make worn here with a striped collared shirt, brown silk tie, leather boots, and original brown felt cloche hat. She's worn a variation of this suit in a myriad of ways, wearing it shooting with a soft collar and tie across the estate, and we also see her at breakfast with just the waistcoat and blouse with crossover collar ready for work.

Lady Mary takes to her role as estate manager at Downton effortlessly and looks stunning in a tailored three-piece suit and tie.

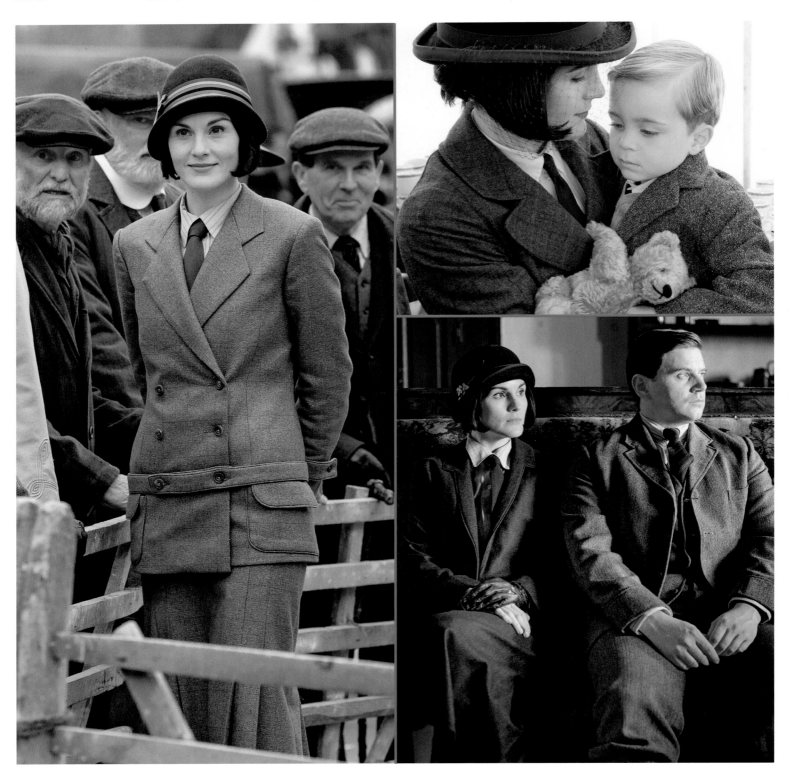

FASHION SHOW

Mary, like her mother and sisters, is generally fashion-forward and ahead of the curve, and in season five attends a fashion show in London with her aunt Rosamund. The outfit she wears, with its dropped waist and fashionable hemline, encapsulated mid-1920s fashion. "This costume feels special," explains Anna Robbins, "as I felt like I'd found the essence of Mary and where I wanted to take her in the second half of the twenties. We were exploring a linear graphic look, with rich primary colors on Lady Mary. It's a bold look for her when paired with a contrasting red hat that exudes confidence and class, and it is still one of my favorite costumes for Mary."

Inspired by a couple of fashion illustrations from the period, the dress was made from contemporary blue silk, with a dropped-waist belt that hugged Mary's hips, and was decorated with hand-finished, jetted buttonholes (a time-consuming process). The contrasting pleated collar and cuffs, made from vintage ivory silk found in Paris, reflected light beautifully. The red felt cloche with upturned brim was accessorized with a Bakelite brooch and curled feather.

At the end of season six, Mary and the family head to Brooklands motor circuit to watch Henry Talbot race. The scene included lots of supporting artists and vintage cars, so, as Anna Robbins explains, "I wanted to make sure Mary stood out against the big crowds both in the stands and on the racetrack. Her interest has been sparked, and because there's this chemistry between her and Henry, I wanted to up the ante a little bit in terms of color and style."

Anna designed a paneled coat for Mary in palest cream, which was set off by a raspberry silk dress, all made in-house using contemporary fabrics. "The look was all about graphic lines, a pale highlight with the coat, and a bold flash of red underneath," says Anna, "but it's also upbeat, fresh, and summery." To accessorize the look, Anna added a bespoke hat, a pair of original gloves, and tortoiseshell sunglasses, the latter in particular giving a real zing to Mary's look as this is the first time we see her in shades. Michelle Dockery makes the most of her sunglasses in the scene, peering over them to view the action beyond.

The bold red and graphic lines of Lady Mary's look at Brooklands is chic and modern, and she and Henry Talbot cut a stylish pair.

ROYAL AUTOMOBILE CLUB

Mary wears this burnt orange evening dress to meet Henry Talbot at the Royal Automobile Club in London. It's a dress that Mary borrows from her aunt Rosamund, so Anna Robbins knew she needed to create something that you could imagine Rosamund wearing but which also works beautifully on Mary.

The workroom first made the copper silk slip to be worn underneath and then created a tiered dress on top with a stunning length of embellished silk tulle from Chez Sarah, a vintage shop in Paris. Anna was drawn to its metallic embroidery, tiny bugle beads, and domed sequins. "I spent ages playing on the stand trying to work out how to layer it," explains Anna, "so it showcased the embroidery and sequins at the right point on the bust, neckline, and hips, and we also added a little lace at the top." The outfit was paired with copper-colored gloves and a beautiful velvet opera coat that Mary shrugs off her shoulders as she enters the club, making quite a statement.

Mary has dinner in London with her new beau, Henry, and borrows a dress from her aunt Rosamund for the occasion.

Mary wears this stunning black-and-gold, fully sequined dress to meet the Hollywood stars and director Jack Barber in *A New Era*. With starbursts of gold sequins on black, this is Mary's version of Hollywood style, and the graphic motifs really suit Mary, who tends not to wear soft floral patterns.

The original dress, which came from Paris, was in near-perfect condition and features an asymmetric hem that is entirely on point for 1928. Hems had risen until 1927, when they were at their shortest, then uneven hems were briefly fashionable until they started to fall again toward the end of the decade.

Mary, who radiates Hollywood glamour in *A New Era*, is joined here by film director Jack Barber, played by Hugh Dancy.

A NEW ERA

Following on from the series, Mary's look in the first *Downton Abbey* movie is graphic and linear, with strength represented by a bold palette. "In *A New Era*, Michelle and I wanted to explore a softer side to Lady Mary," explains Anna Robbins. "Albeit still fashion-forward and a strong woman, and settled in her role running the estate, there is a vulnerability to her that the presence of the film crew and particularly Barber exposes while Henry is away." Mary wore the monochrome look in both movies, which began with an original 1920s collar. The faggoting of the collar was recreated on the cuffs of the blouse and pockets of the waistcoat, which was made out of vintage silk jersey. It

drapes beautifully and created a distinctive and stylish look.

In *A New Era*, the workroom made a dress for Mary in sage green, a new tone for her, side-stepping her usual strong palette of navy blue, deep red, and monochromes. Taking inspiration from a 1928 illustration, the dress is very much looking toward the 1930s, with a fitted belt on the natural waist, which marks a forward shift in style. *Downton* fashion has almost moved full circle, from Edwardian corsetry to dropping the waist and creating a straight, linear look to finding the waist again. Anna knew she wanted Mary to wear this dress in the final scene of the movie—it may be 1928, but the 1930s are on the horizon.

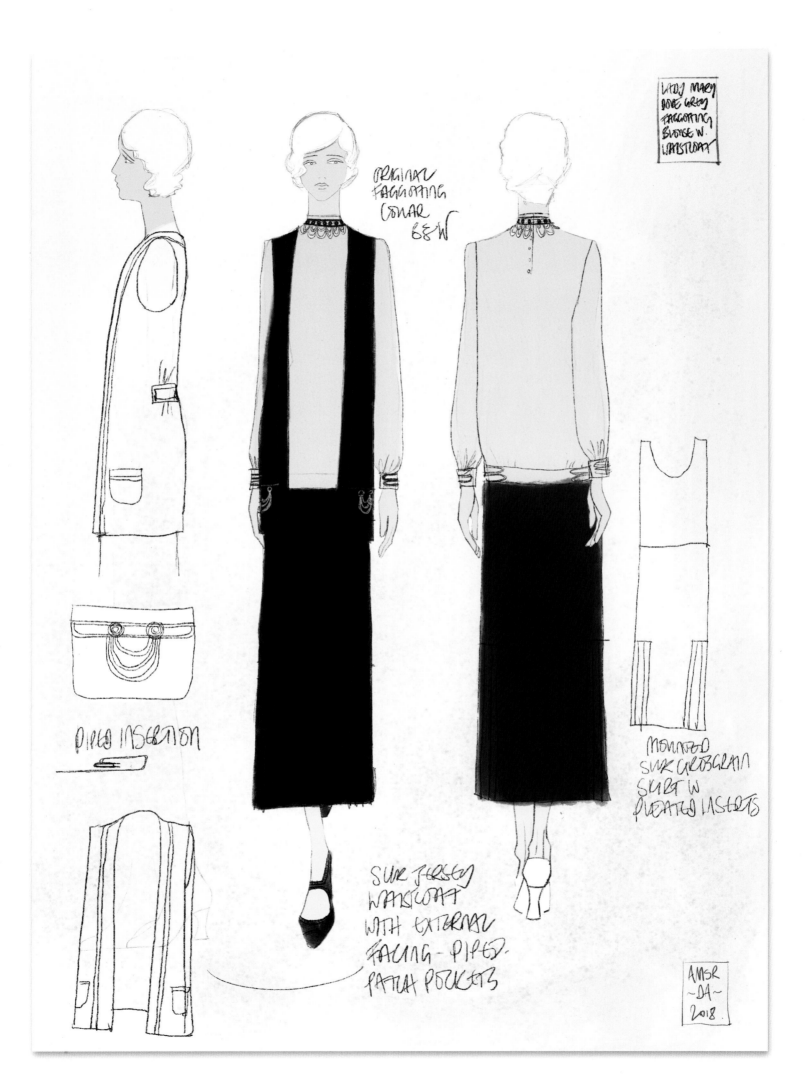

ORIGINAL
FAGGOTING
COLLAR
B&W

LADY MARY
DOVE GREY
FAGGOTING
BLOUSE W.
WAISTCOAT

PIPED INSERTION

MOUNTED
SILK GROSGRAIN
SKIRT W
PLEATED INSERTS

SILK JERSEY
WAISTCOAT
WITH EXTERNAL
FACING - PIPED.
PATCH POCKETS

AMSR
~DA~
2018.

MATTHEW CRAWLEY

Matthew Crawley arrives at Downton Abbey a young, handsome lawyer who has up until that point been living with his mother, Isobel, in Manchester. His life is turned upside down when he discovers he is the heir to the Downton estate, and he initially resists the formalities of aristocratic life, considering them outmoded and stuffy.

When we first meet Matthew, he has the appearance of a smart, working professional, wearing a dark three-piece suit and fedora hat, and he takes to riding a bicycle around the village, much to the consternation of Violet. Despite fearing that the three Crawley sisters would be thrown at him, he and Mary are immediately attracted to each other, and they begin a tumultuous eight-year relationship, finally marrying in 1920.

Matthew becomes increasingly involved in the running of the Downton estate, eventually becoming its co-owner with Lord Grantham. His clothing charts that progression from upper-middle-class lawyer to member of the landed gentry. We see him more frequently in tweeds and evening black and white tie, along with his military uniform during the war years. Lady Mary had long ago fallen for Matthew's good looks and kind nature, and she is devastated when he is killed on the day they welcome their son, George, into the world.

As heir to the Downton estate, Matthew is increasingly seen in earthy-colored tweeds and evening black tie.

HENRY
TALBOT

Henry Talbot is on paper a gentleman, although his prospects, as Lady Mary puts it, are "adequate and not overwhelming," so she initially resists getting too involved despite her obvious attraction to him. Coupled with that, Henry likes to race cars, and having lost Matthew in a car crash, Mary wants to steer clear of any further heartbreak. Henry's considerable charm, however, wins her over, and when he takes Mary to dinner at the RAC Club and the Criterion, they make a very stylish pair. Branson and Violet encourage the union, seeing how right they are for each other, and they eventually marry and go on to have a daughter, Caroline, the following year.

Matthew Goode, who plays Henry, was dressed in original tailoring supplied by Cosprop as well as in bespoke suiting made by Chris Kerr. "Age and a bit of wear sometimes give costumes a bit of life, which really suited Henry, so hired period suiting made sense, punctuated with some sharp, new evening wear," explains Anna Robbins. "Henry is tall and handsome but with a relaxed energy and a languid charm. Matthew Goode looks great in relaxed and formal tailoring, so the process of finding Henry was relatively easy, effortless style coming naturally to both actor and character."

Henry Talbot manages to look debonair in almost anything he wears, from racing car coveralls to black tie and three-piece tweeds (opposite).

COUTURE

The great fashion houses of Europe courted aristocratic women like Cora and Mary, as they had the means to invest in exquisitely made clothing and were in constant need of outfits. In return, the highest quality was assured, and the well-to-do knew they were buying into the very latest fashions, which in turn would filter down to general wear—they were the influencers of the day. The costume designers for *Downton Abbey* also looked to the great couturiers for inspiration, and many of the outfits seen on screen are replicas of influential designs. Some pieces are original, while a handful are very special bespoke makes.

When *Downton Abbey* begins, the Paris-based couturier House of Worth was still a major influence in fashion, although other designers were also emerging, and their more liberated fashions appealed to the younger generation. These included the French fashion designer Paul Poiret, who trained at the House of Worth and whose designs included oriental-style harem pants similar to those worn by Sybil in season one. His influence would be felt throughout the 1920s, with Mary wearing a coat in the first movie inspired by the cut, shape, and appliqué of one of his pieces.

In season three, Caroline McCall created a dress for Mary that is a copy of a design by Madeleine Vionnet, another very famous couturier of the 1920s. Mary wears it on her return from her honeymoon, and the bias cut of the dress with its handkerchief hem—meaning the hem falls in petal points at the bottom—would have been very fashionable in 1920. Vionnet was known for her innovative use of the bias cut, a way of cutting diagonally across the grain of a fabric to create flowing garments that draped over and clung to the natural silhouette of women, encouraging them to dispense with corsets.

Couturier designs influenced many of the fashions in *Downton Abbey*, including those of Madeleine Vionnet who pioneered the bias-cut dress and helped to transform fashion for women.

JEAN PATOU

Parisian designer Jean Patou also had considerable influence in the prewar and postwar eras, with couture collections that moved away from the restrictive clothing of the Edwardian era in favor of dresses without corsets and with free-flowing and shortened skirts. In the 1920s, Patou also created a range of sportswear for women, including knitted jersey swimsuits and tennis wear, and popularized cardigans. His evening dresses were exquisitely made, often in a simple silhouette but with extravagant and intricate beading. In *A New Era,* Mary wears an original Patou dress, which Anna Robbins sourced from a vintage collector. "The chiffon was sadly beginning to perish, so the workroom carefully lifted the beaded body of the dress and remade the bodice, using a certain artistic license to add beading to the neckline, knowing the dress would, for the most part, be worn sat [sitting] down to dinner in the dining room."

In season six, Edith wears what is purported to be an original Patou dress. It is a staggering showcase of the craftmanship of couture in construction and embellishment, which would be near impossible to replicate in the modern day. "The embellishment was so beautiful," explains Anna, "with tiny chain stitch and micro sequins on satin and chiffon. It really was couture at its best, so delicate but with luxurious luster and impact, and so very Edith."

The designs of Mariano Fortuny have also graced the female forms of *Downton Abbey*, with a loan of a handful of original archive pieces and, in collaboration with the heritage company, a couple of bespoke makes. The Spanish-born, Venice-based Mariano Fortuny was a visionary artist and designer, best known in the world of fashion for his distinctive printed textiles and unstructured, opulent gowns. Fortuny's designs were inspired by the past, and his decorative fabrics were heavily influenced by cultures and art from across the globe. He was especially drawn to ancient Greek dress, which led him to develop a modern, unrestricted style of adornment, most famously the iconic Delphos gown.

During season six, Mary wears an original Peplos gown (a Peplos is a two-layered version of the single-layered Delphos), and Lady Rose arrives at Downton in a stunning printed velvet coat. Mary revisits Fortuny for Edith's wedding, wearing a metallic printed dark green coat to the church service. In *A New Era*, Anna Robbins commissioned Fortuny to print a length of mauve velvet in gilded silver for a gown Cora wears to a soiree in the South of France. "We commissioned velvet to be printed by the Fortuny factory in Venice, which we then draped in the *Downton* workroom, having hand pressed it to lie the pile flat, making it panné, which picked up the lights of the party beautifully."

Cora wears a specially commissioned Fortuny dress in *A New Era*, and in season six, Rose and Mary wear original Fortuny pieces in exquisite printed silk and velvet.

LADY MARY NIGHT FIVE

BELT LOOPED
X3 AND DRAPED

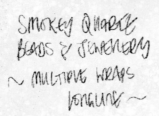

SMOKEY QUARTZ
BEADS & JEWELLERY
~ MULTIPLE WRAPS
LONGLINE ~

MIDNIGHT BLUE SILK
FORTUNY DELPHOS
WITH DEEP V FRONT &
BACK

THE DELPHOS GOWN

Fortuny's most famous creation was arguably the Delphos gown, inspired by the ancient Greek chiton. Developed in 1907 by Fortuny's wife, Henriette, the dress was constructed of fine, hand-pleated silk, to create loose and unrestricted garments but at the same time celebratory of the female form. The resulting gowns skimmed the body's form, allowing for easy movement, and contrasted sharply with the tightly corseted and structured dresses of the Edwardian era. This technique is a heavily guarded secret to this day and has elevated Fortuny's pleated gowns to near mythical status.

Anna first worked with the legendary textile house in season six and then continued to work with them over the years, which led to an opportune collaboration on the first film to create a bespoke pleated gown for Mary. As Anna explains, "This gown is neither vintage nor a replica. It is a 'new' original, with Fortuny having unlocked the famous and secret pleating technique, and is an entirely hand-sewn reimagining of a Delphos gown. The silk was dyed a rich Prussian blue that became glossier and more luminous after pleating. For me, this was the perfect realization of costume and couture."

Lady Mary looks luminous in a bespoke Delphos gown in fine pleated silk, which she wears when entertaining the King and Queen in the first *Downton* film.

EDITH PELHAM

Marchioness of Hexham

Over the years, we have watched Edith's search for happiness, willing her on despite the many setbacks she has suffered along the way. As a young girl, she was unsure of herself and often overshadowed by her more dazzling sisters, which made her a little petulant and awkward at times. But as she navigates adult life, enduring humiliation when left standing at the altar and then the agony of giving up her illegitimate child, she begins to work out her place in the world, building her confidence and eventually finding love in the form of Bertie Pelham.

Along the way, we see an evolution in the way Edith dresses, which reflects her changing circumstances and mindset as well as the new and exciting world in which she lives. During the war, she dons work clothes and jodhpurs for the first time, and in the subsequent years spends more time in London, where she can really flourish, away from her overbearing sister Mary and the confines of life in Yorkshire. The postwar years saw an explosion of popular culture and a crumbling of old social boundaries, and young women like Edith could venture into the city to work or socialize without being chaperoned. Fashions change radically, and Edith embraces the provocative styles, wearing looser, more risqué dresses or shoulder-baring necklines that, as costume designer Caroline McCall puts it, "she would never wear at Downton because they're quite shocking."

With such an evolving journey, the *Downton Abbey* costume designers always enjoyed dressing Edith, none more so than Anna Robbins, as by season six, Edith is really awakened stylistically. "By then she has a career in London, has found happiness with her daughter, and has found her true love. She is really blossoming, so my job was to bring her out."

While Edith undoubtedly becomes more daring in her wardrobe, her costume has never been particularly plain, even in the early seasons of *Downton Abbey*. Susannah Buxton, who established the initial look of all the key characters, didn't want to overplay this side of her and rather let Laura Carmichael, who plays Edith, convey the less appealing side of Edith in her acting. "She may not have looked as dramatic as Mary, but some of Edith's costumes were rather special, and she was often seen in apricots, soft greens, and muted colors, which suited Laura's beautiful complexion."

By season two, during which time war is raging in Europe, evening dress at Downton is a little more somber, and we see Edith wearing a black satin evening gown with silk chiffon overlay and metallic lace hem. The bodice and sleeves are embroidered with pink and gold metallic thread, which gives the dress a soft prettiness. Edith wears it with a pearl pendant necklace and long, pink silk gloves. As this is the mid-1910s, the waist is still fairly high, its silhouette more reminiscent of the late Edwardian era than the linear, looser look of the 1920s.

Susannah Buxton and her team made this dress using a mix of contemporary silk fabrics and original embroidered tulle and metallic lace that was fashioned into the bodice and sleeves.

By the beginning of season four, Edith has embraced London life and meets Michael Gregson at the Criterion restaurant in Piccadilly wearing this striking turquoise beaded dress. While the rest of the family is in mourning over Matthew Crawley's death, Edith has taken a trip to London to meet newspaper editor Michael Gregson, and this marks the first time we see a member of the family wearing any color.

Caroline McCall purposely designed an outfit that would create real impact: "We wanted to see Edith in something completely different and really quite racy, which she could never have worn at home. This is Edith's moment—she is no longer the shrinking vio-let." She even kisses Michael Gregson after he announces his love for her, despite being out in public.

Inspiration for the style of the dress—and the amount of flesh on show—came from a period illustration by French artist George Barbier, and the bodice started life as an original piece of beaded fabric that Caroline had found in Paris. She knew the gold, silver, and pearl beads and sequins would work well in the gold-tiled setting of the Criterion, although the material was in poor repair and needed to be remounted. It was matched with a skirt of turquoise satin and chiffon overlay, but the whole dress was still very delicate and needed a lot of care during and after filming.

Edith wears long, cream satin gloves with her beaded dress, and her bare shoulders make for a racy look in the 1920s.

In season four, Edith wears another halter-neck dress, a style that suits her, as does the peach color, but this dress is a little less revealing and more suitable for wearing at Downton Abbey. The costume team crafted it from an original 1920s dress, which had beautiful beading at the bottom—as was often the case with dresses of the period—but its bodice had perished. Caroline McCall salvaged the skirt and used it for the bodice of Edith's dress—the waist up is obviously more visible on camera, especially if it's a dinner scene—which Caroline then matched with contemporary peach chiffon for the skirt.

Edith's hair, curled in a Marcel wave and worn with a pretty jeweled headpiece and drop earrings, works perfectly with the beading on her dress.

Caroline McCall: "I knew the dress would be Edith's when I bought it. It had a fashionable dropped waist and a longer hemline before they rose to their shortest point in the mid-1920s."

Lady Edith wore this original pale green chiffon dress to Lady Rose's debutante ball at the end of season four. It has a fashionable dropped waist and is embellished with floral metallic embroidery and seed-and-pearl beading. It is also accessorized with a beaded necklace with pendant. The principal female crowd at the ball was designed with gold and silver accents, while Rose wore shocking pink, as she is meant to stand out the most. Lady Edith's dress is in a very delicate shade of green, which suits her character and contrasts well with the dark tailcoats of the men. The dress's metallic embroidery also continues the metallic theme of the female crowd at the ball, and she wears a pretty headpiece in her hair.

The final season of *Downton Abbey* saw Edith continue to blossom as a working woman and business owner, as she becomes more immersed in *The Sketch* magazine, briefly running it herself before she employs a female editor. Her private life also slots into place when she is reunited with her daughter, Marigold, and finds love again with Bertie Pelham. This more positive journey for Edith is reflected in her wardrobe, and we see her in an array of chic working outfits. "It was great to differentiate her London working wardrobe from her life as a lady at Downton Abbey," says Anna Robbins. "To make her more fashion-forward, strengthen her palette, and explore pattern.

"The gray and yellow of this office outfit is one of my favorite looks for Edith. The cape she wears is not only stylish but has a sense of purpose when on the move, as we see Edith leaving her office and walking with Rosamund in a London street. The box pleats and overall proportions for the outfit were inspired by a period illustration, and the cape and skirt were made from gray herringbone wool, which was yellow on the inside so you got a flash of yellow as she walks.

"We matched the suit with a silk collared blouse bound by a pretty floral chiffon, which we also fashioned into a decorative tie, cuffs, and hem. Edith often wears interesting neckwear—leaning toward pussy bows and gathered neckties rather than the more boyish ties and collars that Lady Mary prefers. In fact, I wanted to create unique looks for the two sisters, who were both working women in very different fields, each wearing her own version of a three-piece suit."

Edith finds increasing fulfillment working in London at *The Sketch* magazine offices, and we see her in a variety of stylish outfits.

Edith looks chic when working in her London magazine office, favoring pussy bow neckwear, floaty blouses, and pinafore dresses.

Throughout season six, we see Edith in a variety of London looks. She wears a blue pinafore dress (see below), a blouse with a pleated necktie, and a dark paneled coat when she bumps into Bertie, who then comes to her aid when she has to work through the night at *The Sketch* magazine office. The coat is an original made of paneled grosgrain silk, whereby the technique of placing the panels in different directions means the grain of the fabric reacts to light in varying ways. Edith wears the coat on other occasions in the season, including on a parasoled stroll through the grounds of Downton Abbey.

Opposite: Edith wears this original 1920s cornflower blue beaded dress to Bertie's family home of Brancaster Castle. As some of the original beading had perished, Anna Robbins and her team had to carefully re-bead sections. They also added a long chiffon slip to make the dress floor-length.

Beautiful cornflower blue becomes Edith, as this beaded floor-length evening gown (opposite) illustrates, but she also continues to embrace bolder hues as the series progresses. Below she wears a petrol-blue jacket with matching vest, hand embroidered with multicolored cross-stitch. Embroidered garments were fashionable in the 1920s, partly as a result of émigrés from revolutionary Russia who had set up couture houses in Paris, bringing with them Russian-style embroidery. The items originally formed part of a three-piece set with pajama-styled pants, as sourced by Anna Robbins, and while pajama sets are featured in *A New Era*, it was far too early to introduce them in season six, set in 1925. So instead she matched them with a pleated, cream wool skirt to create a coordinated ensemble befitting the Downton setting.

In the first movie, Edith and Bertie, who married in season six, arrive at Downton Abbey with daughter Marigold. They are the Marquess and Marchioness of Hexham now, but they are still a modern couple, happy to travel without a nanny or valet. "It's 1927," announces Bertie. "We're modern folk." Anna Robbins built Edith's ensemble around an original chiffon blouse featuring delicate peach and navy wool embroidery. She says, "With Edith, an interesting textile is often a starting point. Be that embroidery, beading, print, or a crocheted silk knit, there is usually something beautiful about the textiles she wears. Edith tops the blouse with a vintage terra-cotta silk grosgrain coat with inlaid paneling, and she dons a cloche hat with upturned brim that matches the blue of her gloves and fashionably short skirt, which hits just below her knees."

Edith wore another fine example of 1920s beading for the royal dinner hosted by the Crawley family at Downton. The dress was in mint condition, of French origin, and beaded on muslin, so it was relatively strong. The workroom added a georgette slip to mirror the hemline and extend the length of the dress. Edith wears the dress with a several-stranded necklace, long silver gloves, and a stunning starburst bandeau tiara, positioned low on her forehead. "While her tiara is a modern replica," explains Anna, "it's a wonderful re-creation of how pretty and fun tiaras and hair adornments could be."

Edith wears this slender, peach-colored dress in the first and second movies. It is embroidered with glass beading—typical of 1920s dresses—and also features an undulating hem that was very fashionable in 1928.

From beautifully embroidered textiles to exquisitely beaded dresses, Edith embraces the modern styles of the 1920s.

PALAZZO PANTS

In *A New Era*, Edith travels to the south of France with some of the Crawley family and household. Edith continues to make bold sartorial choices in her clothing, and this trip is the perfect excuse to explore the fashions sported by the famous artists and writers who are holidaying there. Not only does she wear a printed three-piece pajama set in ivory and jade—which was all the rage on the French Riviera in the late 1920s—but she also dons wide-legged palazzo pants with a matching vest. This is worn under an original art deco–printed jacket in peach, cobalt blue, and emerald green, with a headscarf, jade beads, and T-bar shoes to complete the look. It's a strikingly stylish, relaxed look on Edith, and perfect for vacationing in the South of France.

* JADE JEWELS

LADY
EDITH
RIVIERA
PALAZZO

SILK FABRIC
VENTED BUTTON
HOLES

ORIGINAL 1920s
PEACH COBALT &
GREEN DECO PRINT
KIMONO JACKET

WIDE LEG IVORY
CREPE SILK TRS.
SINGLE FRONT
PLEATS

MATCHING SOFT V
VEST WITH MINIMAL
EXCESS TO TACK.

TWO TONE
CREAM & IVORY
DBL STRAP MARY JANE

AMSR
~DA~
2018.

BERTIE PELHAM

Marquess of Hexham

When Edith first meets Bertie Pelham, he's a land agent for Brancaster Castle and a distant cousin to the incumbent Marquess Lord Hexham. Bertie is instantly smitten by Edith, and from the outset, there is an ease between the pair. Edith, however, resists telling Bertie the truth about her daughter, Marigold, and only when that matter is sorted out can they move ahead and marry. Bertie has also unexpectedly inherited the Marquess of Brancaster title, but the rise in rank doesn't go to his head, and he remains as level-headed, honest, and charming as ever.

Bertie, as is to be expected of a man of his standing, is perfectly at ease in both a tweed suit and formal white tie. Harry was quite happy to wear traditional tailoring, including a stiff-collared shirt and waistcoat, because, as he put it, "it informed how I moved," helping him to stand and sit up straight as was required of gentlemen in polite company. Things were, however, changing a little on this front, as Harry explains: "In 1925, gentlemen were on the cusp of being allowed to cross their legs when seated. In a scene in Edith's office, we did a cheeky cross leg—we decided that as I was away from home, it would be all right."

Bertie Pelham is used to formalwear and has a relaxed air about him whether he's dressing for dinner or wearing a daytime suit.

THE GREAT WAR

S eason two of *Downton Abbey* opens in November 1916, amid the mud-strewn trenches of the First World War. The conflict, which sees members of the Downton household fighting on the front line, imbues much of the season, with those left at home united in the war effort. Military uniforms take center stage throughout the season, and Lord Grantham feels very much at home in the formal mess uniform of the Grenadier Guards, which he wears for a large regimental dinner held at Downton Abbey. He has, of course, seen active service before, principally in the Second Boer War (1899–1902), where Bates served as his batman, and he takes pride in having fought for King and Country.

Prior to the regimental dinner, he had received an invitation to take up the position of colonel of the local volunteers, and, as actor Hugh Bonneville puts it, "The soldier in him is reawakened, and he's itching to get back into active service, to join the club, the gang again." His hopes, however, are dashed when he discovers his role as colonel is an honorary position befitting his age and rank.

Overseeing the many uniforms and clothing of the season was costume designer Rosalind Ebbutt, and one of her key tasks was to dress the large numbers of senior-ranking officers attending the regimental dinner. The costumiers Angels, which has a dedicated military department, made many of the costumes. Robert's mess uniform was copied from a 1912 original worn by an officer serving in India. It consists of a scarlet Melton wool tunic with navy collar and cuffs, a navy wool waistcoat with brass regimental buttons, navy dress tunic trousers with wide scarlet stripe, a stiff-fronted shirt with wing-tipped collar, and a black bow tie. Susannah Buxton designed this suit in dark red with matching cloche hat to create a striking silhouette for this significant scene.

The costume department also had the help of Major General Alastair Bruce, a senior reservist of the British Army and historical advisor to *Downton Abbey*. During filming, Alastair paid close attention to every detail on the uniforms to ensure they carried the correct badges of rank, medals, and various insignia appropriate to the era.

Below: Lord Grantham, in his regimental mess uniform, wears a row of miniature medals on his lapel. (Opposite) We see the Queen Victoria and Edward VII Boer War medals with campaign clasps, and coronation medals for King Edward VII and King George V, as presented to members of the armed forces present at the coronation ceremonies in 1902 and 1911, respectively.

Fighting at the front line are Matthew Crawley and Thomas Barrow, who are caught up in the Battle of the Somme in 1916, where almost half a million British soldiers lost their lives. Amid gunfire and explosions, they face the full horror of trench warfare, a world away from the genteel life of Downton Abbey.

For the battle scene, we see Matthew and Thomas in their khaki ("drab" in military speak) uniforms and steel Brodie helmets. To film the scene, which was shot in a series of trenches in Suffolk, the principal actors, Dan Stevens and Rob James-Collier, were joined by supporting artists and specialist First World War reenactors, some of whom brought their own uniforms for filming. The costumiers Angels supplied all the other uniforms, which the costume department covered in real mud prior to shooting.

Thomas has joined the war as a medic, and the arm of his tunic bears two stripes to denote his corporal rank (he would later be promoted to lance sergeant) and the red cross of the Royal Army Medical Corps, which approved its use in filming. Matthew Crawley would have started his career as an officer, beginning as a lieutenant and rising to captain, his rank signified by two or three stars on his shoulder.

Away from the front line and back at Downton Abbey, we see Matthew and Thomas in their khaki uniforms, both in peaked caps. Matthew wears leather field boots, a Sam Browne belt and supporting strap, and braids known as aiguillettes. He also wears a shirt with a soft collar and tie, whereas Thomas wears a collarless gray serge shirt and a tunic made from coarser fabric buttoned up to the neck. Thomas wears puttees, strips of cloth that wound around the legs to seal boots, keeping everything dry. Rob James-Collier enjoyed wearing his puttees, commenting that he found his wartime uniform far more comfortable than the stiff neck collar he was usually required to wear as a footman.

To add an extra layer of detail to the uniforms, regiments were created: the Duke of Manchester's Own for Matthew and the North Riding Volunteers for Lord Grantham. The College of Arms, overseen by Alastair Bruce, created drawings of their crests, which were then used for regimental badges, as seen on cap badges and lapels, and cleared for use by the army.

Back on the home front, the impact of war could be felt everywhere, including in the everyday dress of women. Most visible were the vast army of women who took up war work—by the end of the war, almost a million women were involved in munitions—and they needed to wear practical clothes, without the restrictions of long skirts or tight corsets. While aristocratic types like the Crawley family may have thought life would continue much as before, they too were affected, and we see some of the household dressed in a way once considered unthinkable just a year or two before.

Many of the rituals at Downton Abbey continue, and the family still dress in finery for dinner, but as Michelle Dockery, who plays Lady Mary, noticed, the style of clothing felt a little more relaxed in the season, her skirts less constrained, with a little ankle beginning to show. Some of the upstairs ladies may not have changed outfits quite as much as they did before the war, and extravagant jewelry or feathers in the hair would have been deemed a little inappropriate as war raged in Europe.

Some of the women at Downton are determined to make themselves useful, including Edith, who chooses to work on a farm—as did some twenty-three thousand women who joined the Women's Land Army. In doing so, Edith learns to drive a tractor, and for the first time, we see her in breeches and jodhpurs, working jackets, and knee-length boots. Edith can now move and sit in a more casual way, although she still wears a day corset, having not quite dispensed fully with the Edwardian way of doing things.

Costume designer Rosalind Ebbutt also needed to be mindful of the overall palette in scenes, which meant creating costumes that worked well with the khaki and scarlet-red uniforms. Throughout the season, there is something of a "red, white, and blue" feel to many of the group scenes, and Rosalind and the costume team looked to dress the ladies in colors—deep reds and velvety blues—that worked well alongside the uniforms' colors. Season one costume designer Susannah Buxton also designed for cast members in season two, including the scene when Mary sees Matthew off at the station. She made Mary a suit and hat in a claret color that worked beautifully with the khaki uniforms on the platform setting, while making Mary a striking figure in an emotionally charged scene.

Edith enjoys working as a land girl, and Laura Carmichael, who plays Edith, loved the new look: "I got to wear trousers—it was exciting!"

Sybil has always been driven to do something meaningful with her life, and the outbreak of war gives her a prime opportunity. She takes on the role of nurse, large numbers of which were needed to see to the wounded soldiers coming off the front line. She receives rudimentary training in York, joining the Voluntary Aid Detachment, or VADs, as they were known, many of whom were middle- or upper-class women, as there was no pay. It was nonetheless a challenging job, with nurses often called upon to perform, in addition to their lighter duties of bed making, such difficult tasks as tending to men who had lost limbs or endured other terrible injuries.

The uniform Sybil wears for work at Downton Abbey is a long gray dress with a white apron, cuffs, headdress, and soft collar. Fortunately for Jessica Brown Findlay, the actress who plays Sybil, the uncomfortable stiff-backed collars had been phased out by 1916. On her arm, she wears a red cross, although her uniform differs from the official Red Cross uniforms worn by the real VADs of the time. They wore blue dresses and a white armband with a red cross. Sybil's dress was purposely made in gray with a red cross on a gray band on her arm.

Sybil uses her new nursing skills at Downton Abbey when it is set up as a convalescent home for wounded soldiers. Isobel and Cora oversee the hospital, and Mary also helps out and tends to Matthew after he is badly injured in the war.

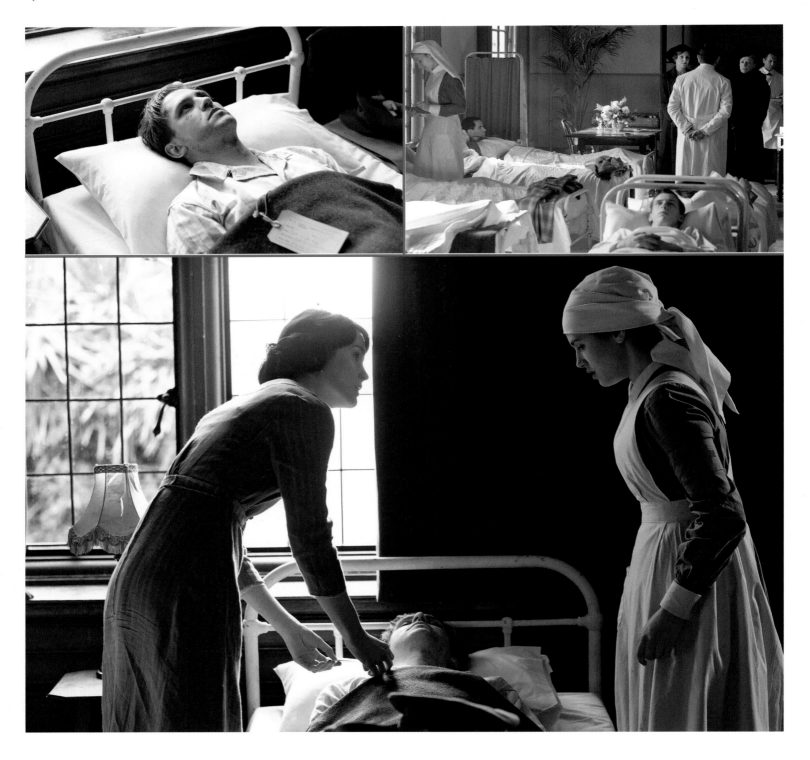

LADY SYBIL
CRAWLEY

Lady Sybil Crawley was the youngest daughter of the Earl and Countess of Grantham. Sweet-natured and compassionate, Sybil was also something of a rebel, interested in socialist ideals and equality for women and less concerned about her aristocratic place in the world. The clothes she wore were largely befitting of her class, and as a natural beauty, she looked exquisite in them. But she was drawn to a bohemian style of dress and less accepting of social conventions. She had previously questioned why women bothered with corsets: "Men don't wear them and they look perfectly normal in their clothes." Her sisters were quick to ridicule her viewpoint: "She's just showing off. She'll be on about the vote in a minute."

In season one, Sybil shocked the family when she arrived downstairs for dinner wearing blue harem trousers. It made for an arresting sight, as in the years before the First World War, no woman, particularly of the aristocratic class, would ever have been seen in trousers. Sybil's intention was, of course, to shock, to rebel against the social expectations of her gender and class, and to advertise in a very visual sense her affiliation to the suffragette cause.

Sybil's harem trousers were resonant of the Eastern design influences sweeping through Europe, triggered by the tour of the Ballets Russes, an itinerant ballet company that arrived in London in 1911 and put on shows notable for their opulent, daring costumes. The French designer Paul Poiret was inspired by the gorgeous spectacle and began to design revolutionary new forms of women's dress, including oriental jupe-culottes and decorated turbans. For women like Lady Sybil, who are keen to move away from the tightly corseted and restricting skirts of ladies' dress, these looks represent female liberation and a changing world.

For costume designer Susannah Buxton, Sybil's harem trousers mark an important moment in the season. The family are left waiting for Sybil, knowing that she's wearing a new "dress," only for her to stun them all with her new evening attire. The outfit was crafted by

Susannah and her team using a delicate organza net with gold thread for the sleeves and a panel of original embroidery sourced from a vintage fair for the beautiful peacock bodice. The two-toned turquoise pantaloons were made from layers of blue silk chiffon sourced at Shepherd's Bush Market in London with a paler chiffon on top. The diamanté and metallic embroidered headpiece is an original from the period, and Sybil also wears an Egyptian-inspired bronze-and-pearl necklace.

The filming of scenes for *Downton Abbey* often requires multiple takes, and Sybil's peacock bodice began to split at the back as the camera rolled. "Fortunately, we did have another piece of it," says Susannah, "but watching a dress part from itself in front of your eyes on camera is pretty scary."

Sybil's blue harem trousers made for a memorable scene in *Downton Abbey* and were met with shock by the family.

In season three, Sybil has married Tom Branson and is now carrying their child. She wears this gray velvet dress a few times; unlike her sisters, she doesn't feel the need to wear multiple outfits, and she can wear it while pregnant. The bohemian feel of the dress, with its arts and crafts–style embroidery, also suits Sybil. (Floral, natural motifs were a feature of arts and crafts design, which also promoted looser, less restrictive clothing for women.)

The dress was an original made by the house of Vitaldi Babani, a couturier based in Paris. The fashion house originally imported exotic goods, selling Japanese kimonos and garments by Fortuny and Liberty, before specializing in its own designs, typically in silk velvet with beautifully handcrafted embroideries. When Caroline McCall found the dress, much of the top and body had perished, leaving just the embroidery, which the costume team remounted on silk velvet dyed to match the original dress.

Sadly, this is one of the last few dresses we see Sybil wear as, shockingly, after giving birth, she began to experience fits due to eclampsia, which led to her death. Her daughter was named Sybil, and the family and Tom were deeply affected by her loss.

Sybil looks beautiful and fresh-faced during her pregnancy, and her death after childbirth is a tragedy.

ROYAL GUESTS

Lord and Lady Grantham are used to welcoming eminent guests to Downton Abbey, and there are none more illustrious than King George and Queen Mary, who pay them a visit in the first movie as part of their tour of Yorkshire. They bring with them a large retinue of household staff, and the royal party is later joined by their daughter, Princess Mary, who lives nearby.

As executive producer Gareth Neame commented, "It is fun to have the fictional characters of *Downton* merge with the real world"—and the King and Queen are, of course, based on the real King George V, who ascended the throne in 1910, and his queen consort, Mary of Teck. It was the job of the actors (Simon Jones and Geraldine James) to embody the royal couple, with the help of hair, makeup, and the costume team, who researched extensively and put a huge amount of work into their visual transformation.

"There are, of course, a huge amount of pictorial references for the King and Queen, so we could pick up on really fine details," explains Anna Robbins. "When it came to the King, for example, we could home in on the watch chain and cuff links he wore, along with the type of cravats or stiff collars he favored. He was very particular about the cut of his trousers and how he wore them. He disapproved of having a crease down the middle of trousers, and it enraged him when his sons wore them that way, so we made sure we prepared and pressed his suits the right way.

"Similarly, when it came to the Queen's costumes, I looked at countless photos of the Queen with John Bright at Cosprop, analyzing the cut and construction of her clothing along with what kind of material might have been used and finished—really taking it down to stitch detail. In our initial meeting, John brought out dresses from his personal collection that had belonged to the Queen herself. It was astonishing—and such a unique privilege to be able to handle and to see the garments and really understand how they were constructed, and to see the embellishments up close."

Geraldine James was also amazed to see original dresses of Queen Mary: "They were incredibly delicate and beautiful, and I actually got to hold one of the dresses. I can't tell you how exciting that was." Geraldine attended long hours of costume fittings and, to match the distinctive silhouette of Queen Mary, wore bespoke padding underneath her corset.

King George V and Queen Mary, played by Simon Jones and Geraldine James, bore the distinctive look of the real King and Queen.

At the royal ball featured in the first film, Queen Mary wears a stunning gown that closely resembles the formal dress the historic queen would have worn to such an event. It also marked one of Anna Robbins's favorite design journeys: "My starting point was a piece of incredible silver metallic lace that ended up forming the draped overskirt of the dress. John Bright from Cosprop upped the ante with a beautiful piece of antique beaded cobweb lace that became the bodice and sleeves, and then dug out from his treasure trove a roll of beautiful silver lamé that had once belonged to Queen Mary herself. And so it came to pass that the underskirt of Geraldine's costume had a direct link back to the woman she was playing. It was quite a moment."

The Queen also wears replicas of the famed Cambridge Emeralds and Vladimir Tiara, a parure of jewelry that her late Majesty Queen Elizabeth II wore frequently. Anna Robbins purposely wanted the royal ensemble to wear recognizable royal jewels as a way of rooting them in reality.

Queen Mary's ceremonial decoration includes the sash of the Order of the Garter, the Lesser George, the diamond Garter Star, and a diamond garter on her arm. The Order of the Garter is the most prestigious order of chivalry worn by royalty and no more than twenty-four living people. The Queen also wears the Imperial Order of the Crown of India (as she is the Empress of India), the Royal Order of Victoria and Albert, and the Royal Family Order of George V. The King's decoration was even more impressive, boasting the garter sash with the Lesser George, a diamond Most Noble Order of the Garter Breast Star, and the Order of the Garter around his left leg alongside his miniature medals, which comprised twenty-three individual elements that all needed to be sourced or custom-made as replicas.

Princess Mary, played by Kate Phillips, wears a customized original ivory velvet ball gown with silver thread embroidery and seed pearl decoration. Her ceremonial adornment includes the Imperial Order of the Crown of India, the Royal Family Order of George V, and the sash, breast star, and medal of the Most Excellent Order of the British Empire. She also wears diamond and pearl jewelry and a diamond fringe tiara that is a replica of the one that was gifted to Princess Mary by her mother. (The Fringe Tiara was famously worn by Queen Elizabeth II on her wedding day and was subsequently worn by Princess Anne in 1973 and Princess Beatrice in 2020.)

Henry Lascelles, Earl of Harewood, Princess Mary, King George V, and Queen Mary wear ceremonial sashes and formal evening attire.

QUEEN MARY ~ 116 ROYAL BAL.

DOWNTON
ABBEY 203
A. M. S. R.

CAMBRIDGE EMERALDS
VLADIMIR TIARA.

SILVER METALLIC LACE
DRAPED CROSS OVER
WITH BEADED COBWEB LACE
SLEEVES, BODICE —
SILVER LAMÉ SKIRTS WITH
ORGANZA OVERLAY

SILK & TULLE INFIL
RUCHED STAND COLLAR

RUCHED ONTO HIP

- SASH ORDER OF GARTER
- LESSER GEORGE
- DIAMOND GARTER STAR
- DIAMOND GARTER (LH)
- IMP. ORDER CROWN INDIA
- ROYAL ORDER V&A
- ROYAL FAMILY ORDER
  GEORGE V.

INSPECTING THE TROOPS

The first *Downton Abbey* movie also features a magnificent parade of the Yorkshire Hussars in the village, after which the King on horseback inspects the troops. The royal guests, along with the Crawley family, view the procession from a raised dais, the ladies in day wear and hats, the King in full dress uniform, and Lord Grantham in his lord lieutenant's uniform.

For Queen Mary, Anna Robbins recreated as faithfully as possible a look from a well-known photograph of the Queen consisting of a dove-gray wool coat with fur-trimmed collar, scalloped caped sleeves, and a high-necked ivory lace infill, which she accessorized with a pearl brooch, earrings, and necklace, and a pleated-silk toque hat. Queen Mary favored the toque, a hat with no brim and often pleated and adorned with a plume or feather, and wore one throughout much of her adult life. This sat on top of a mass of tightly waved hair, all of which added to Queen Mary's rather imposing look.

King George's field marshal full dress uniform consists of mess uniform, cocked hat, black leather boots, and white gloves. With some fifty-two elements, the King's costume is one of the most complex costumes ever recreated for *Downton Abbey*. The tailoring is bespoke, with gold bullion embroidery by Hand & Lock, and the hat and boots are custom-made. And with advice from Alastair Bruce, the costume department pulled together all the decoration, including the King's full-size medal set (he wears a full-size set at the parade and miniatures at the ball). As with the King's evening decoration, the costume department sourced originals where possible and replicated parts if they were uniquely worn by the King himself.

The clothing worn by Geraldine James was modeled on the real Queen Mary who is pictured here sitting next to a young Princess Elizabeth. The King (opposite) sits astride his horse in full mess uniform complete with a set of full-size medals, the Most Noble Order of the Garter Breast Star, amongst other insignia.

ISOBEL GREY

Lady Merton

Isobel, played by Penelope Wilton, first meets the Crawley family when her son, Matthew, becomes heir to the Downton Abbey estate. She is from an upper-middle-class background, the daughter of a doctor and widow to Dr. Reginald Crawley, Lord Grantham's third cousin. The aristocratic world she finds herself in is alien to both her and her son, although Isobel navigates it very well, despite the odd clash with Violet. Isobel is intelligent, resourceful, and a trained nurse, and involves herself in a variety of worthwhile causes at Downton, among them working at the village hospital. She is forward-thinking and liberal, and her clothing moves with the times, albeit in a more understated way, suitable for a woman of her age and place in society.

If working, Isobel will wear practical, unfussy clothes, but she'll dress in rich colors and elegant textiles, her outfits considered and appropriate to the occasion. In earlier seasons, her skirts are always floor-length and her sleeves long—her silhouette not unlike that of Mrs. Hughes, the housekeeper—although her hems rise to ankle-length in later seasons and stay there, and she favors wide-brimmed hats over her swept-up hair. Reds like carmine, maroon, and burgundy work well on her, as do blues in vivid navy or soft, smoky tones, illustrated here by the misty blue suit she wears to her son's wedding to Mary and which she also wears to a garden party later in the season. For a practical woman like Isobel, she no doubt would ensure to get more than one wear out of most of her clothing.

Isobel's mother-of-the-groom outfit is made up of a belted two-piece suit in blue wool crepe with a shawl collar trimmed with detailed Chinese embroidery and worn with a delicate lace panel infill. Caroline McCall, who designed the outfit, explains, "I wanted Isobel to look smart and yet still practical, and the style of the suit would have been fashionable in the late teens." Chinoiserie, as reflected in Isobel's embroidered collar, became something of a craze in fashion in the 1920s, so her look is both current but also appropriate for the mother of the groom. The costume team also made a straw-brimmed hat to match the dress, with a pleated band and ivory buckle and a spray of blue-gray feathers.

Isobel wears a pretty blue suit with embroidered collar to Matthew and Mary's wedding and also to afternoon tea later in the season.

By the time of her only son Matthew's death, Isobel is fully embedded in life at Downton Abbey and in the village. She never expected to marry again, but she is introduced to the widower Lord Merton, and after a protracted courtship, they eventually marry. Lord Merton is a bona fide aristocrat, and while Isobel still retains her signature look and style, elements of her clothing and accessories reflect her upward mobility. "When Isobel marries Merton, her financial circumstances and position within society change," explains Anna Robbins, "and we reflected that by using more sumptuous fabrics. We repurposed some vintage fur for a collar to add a touch of luxury. Such little touches elevated her clothing, although Isobel as a character doesn't change."

When the royal family visit Downton Abbey, Isobel looks resplendent in a beaded velvet tunic-cut dress—a simple, elegant cut that always suited her—with a boatneck and long sleeves. She and Lord Merton look every inch the grandee couple.

When it came to hats, Isobel continued to favor a wide-brimmed style, perhaps in felt or straw, often with an asymmetric upturned brim. "We experimented with smaller brims as a nod toward the changing tide of fashion, but they didn't work as well, and we felt a softer, wider brim suited Isobel's sense of style," explains Anna. "There were an infinite number of ways to adapt this signature look through fabric, color, and trim." Isobel's outfits often complemented the more Edwardian look of Violet's clothing, the two ladies spending increasing time with each other.

Isobel and Violet take a walk in the grounds of Downton Abbey. The red of Isobel's coat works well with Violet's gray outfit, which seems more dated.

LORD
MERTON

Lord Merton is an old friend of the Crawleys, godfather to Lady Mary, and a widower when he meets Isobel Crawley. Despite their differences—he has an aristocratic upbringing, and Isobel is very much upper middle class—the pair are drawn to each other, and he admires Isobel's inquiring mind, medical knowledge (having once wished to be a doctor himself), and progressive outlook. His two sons and daughter-in-law deem Isobel beneath them, but Lord Merton is undeterred, and Isobel eventually accepts his proposal of marriage.

Lord Merton, played by Douglas Reith, cuts a handsome figure, and his suits, whether they are three-piece check tweeds or white tie, seem to fit him like a glove. Lord Merton's suiting came from the costume houses of Cosprop and Angels, with some choice bespoke tailoring. With Isobel by his side, he looks content, far more than he ever was with his previous wife, Ada.

LADY ROSAMUND PAINSWICK

Lady Rosamund Painswick, sister to Lord Grantham, lives in Belgrave Square, London, where she once lived with her wealthy late husband, Sir Marmaduke Painswick. Without any children of her own, she is close to Robert and her nieces, and is a frequent visitor to Downton Abbey. With easy access to the culture and society of the capital, including its fashion shows and couturiers, Rosamund dresses exquisitely, and her look is always striking, her hair intricately styled in the latest fashion.

Designing for Rosamund was something of a gift for Downton's costume department. As a character, she breezes in and out of the series, so she can often get away with bolder looks or colors. Samantha Bond, who plays Rosamund, could wear many of the vintage pieces sourced for her, and season one designer Susannah Buxton soon realized that Samantha could really "work" an outfit during filming: "If a dress she was wearing had an unusual sleeve, then she might lean against a door with her arm raised just to ensure the sleeves were caught on camera."

Dramatic hats are also a key part of Rosamund's look. Whether it's a large-brimmed style or a more upright toque, she wears them with flair. In season six, for Mary's wedding to Matthew, Anna Robbins designed

a wide-brimmed hat for Rosamund, which she upturned on one side to give it a dramatic shape from every side. Its contrast trim matched her two-piece dress, and a red rose picked up the deco rose print, as well as its red fringing and bead necklace.

Rosamund can also wear quite unusual colors, such as copper, which complements her auburn hair and green eyes, as well as black, which was a fashionable color in the 1920s, although the costume department used it sparingly on other characters, unless they were in mourning. In season five she arrives at Downton wearing a daytime outfit in an unusual chartreuse green, with a green silk toque.

Rosamund always welcomes her nieces and younger relatives to London, where they are less confined by the demands put on them at Downton Abbey and can experiment a little in their dress. Rose, of course, takes this to an extreme when she dons a flapper dress and sneaks off to a jazz club, forcing Rosamund to hunt her down. In general, however, Rosamund supports her nieces through difficult times, keeping Edith's pregnancy a secret and escorting her to Switzerland for the birth. But she can be quite hard-edged in her advice, a little snobbish, and she lacks the sentimentality of her brother.

Lady Rosamund, played by Samantha Bond, often wears eye-catching, complementary outfits in the very latest London styles.

To meet the family solicitor, Mr. Murray, in *A New Era*, Rosamund wore an original beaded dress, to which the costume department added sleeves. "She has now fully moved away from the corseted look," explains Anna Robbins, "and did so fairly early on, even though she's the same generation as Robert. Her silhouette now is very linear, but a dropped waist at the hip is hinted at in the dress pattern."

Later on in the movie, Rosamund is costumed in an evening dress of petrol-blue satin with long, matching velvet waistcoat, a color that looks incredible on Rosamund with her hair and complexion. The waistcoat is vintage with decorative glass beading, and the look is set off with statement jet, diamond, and jade jewelry that was very of the period.

Dark colors also look good on Rosamund, and she wears more black, which was very on trend in the 1920s, than other characters in *Downton Abbey*.

BOUDOIR AND UNDERWEAR

O ver the course of *Downton Abbey,* we often see characters in their bedrooms, particularly the upstairs family who are dressed and undressed by lady's maids or valets, or served breakfast in bed (as was the preserve of married women like Cora). Here they can have more private conversations, and over the years, we've glimpsed an array of nightgowns and underclothes.

In the filming of such scenes, costume designers need to be mindful of the practicalities of dressing or undressing on camera. Dialogue can still be exchanged while lady's maid Anna tightens Mary's corset, or Mr. Bates slips a waistcoat onto Lord Grantham, but elegantly removing a dress is more of a challenge. In a bedroom scene in season six, Anna helps Lady Mary out of a black dress, which drops to the ground as they talk (rather than Anna having to pull it over her head), revealing Mary's silk underwear. "I had to design a dress that could be undone on camera, dropping to the ground in a puddle of silk," explains costume designer Anna Robbins.

Both the silk kimono and nightgown worn by Lady Mary were original pieces sourced by Anna Robbins. "I always loved the opportunity to costume the *Downton* women in nightgowns and dressing gowns for the bedroom scenes because there are such beautiful originals to be found. I would pay careful attention to the palette of the room and pick patterns and tones to complement the setting. We see kimonos across the *Downton* series. Imported from Japan, they were initially used as dressing gowns, and their fabric and shape became a great source of inspiration for couture designers in Paris."

Underneath the kimono Lady Mary wears a bias-cut nightgown of ivory silk with handworked embroidery.

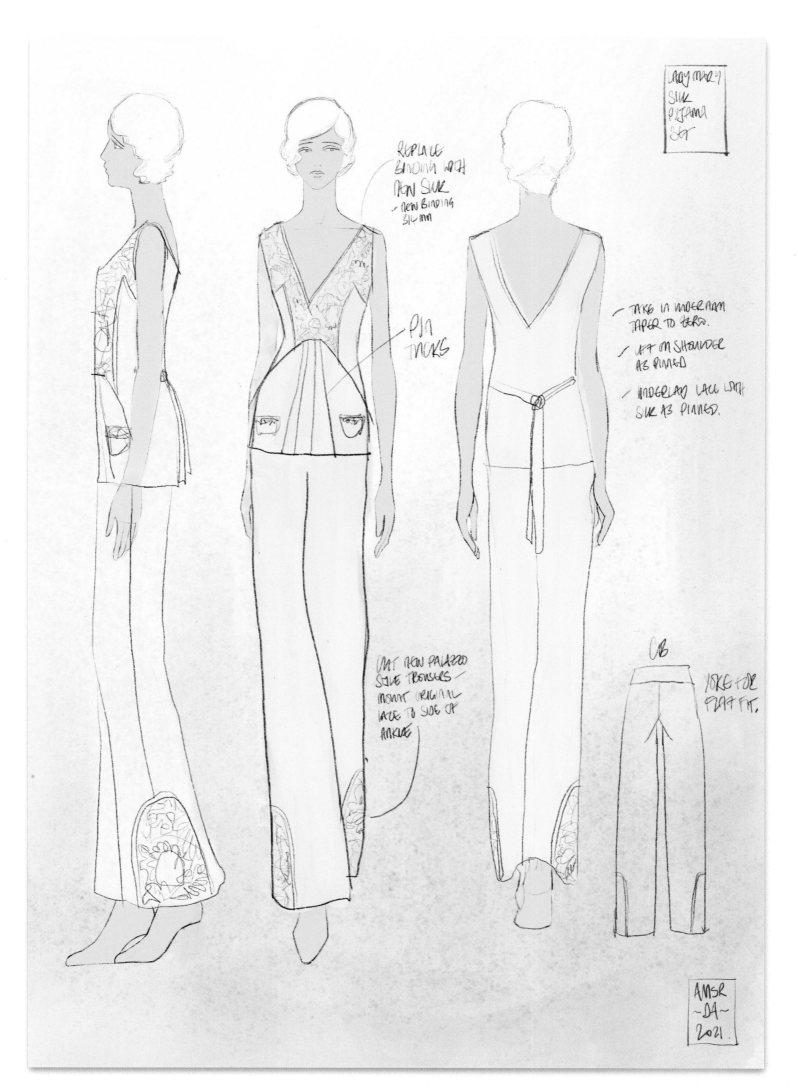

REPLACE
BINDING WITH
NEW SILK
- NEW BINDING
SILK mm

PIN
TUCKS

LADY MARY
SILK
PYJAMA
SET

TAKE IN UNDERARM
TAPER TO ZERO.

LIFT ON SHOULDER
AS PINNED

UNDERLAY LACE WITH
SILK AS PINNED.

CB

YOKE FOR
FLAT FIT.

DART NEW PALAZZO
STYLE TROUSERS —
MOUNT ORIGINAL
LACE TO SIDE OF
ANKLE

AMSR
~DA~
2021.

"We also had the opportunity to make
some beautiful sets of underwear for
Lady Mary and Lady Edith using
original lace and contemporary
silk satin, engineering looks that
blended period correctness with
the requirements of underwear on set."

—ANNA ROBBINS

LADY ROSE MacCLARE

Lady Rose MacClare, the great-niece of the Dowager Countess, is a frequent visitor to Downton Abbey and comes to stay with the Crawley family while her parents are in India. Born in 1902, she is young and fun-loving and fully embraces the new fashions and changing culture of post-war Britain in the 1920s. She is also attracted to the bright lights of London and likes nothing more than to dance the night away in glittery flapper-style dresses.

While Lady Rose is something of a wild spirit, she is still expected to be formally introduced into London society as a debutante, with Cora, Countess of Grantham, officially hosting her season. The aristocratic ritual involved presenting well-born young ladies to the reigning monarch so they could "come out" into society and attend debutante balls and parties where they could meet eligible young men. In the case of Rose, she attends the first presentation in 1923 after an enforced hiatus during the First World War and is presented to King George V and Queen Mary at Buckingham Palace. (At her later ball, she dances with the Prince of Wales,

the future King Edward VIII, which is viewed as a huge honor for a young debutante.)

Etiquette and clothing worn to a presentation at court followed a very specific set of rules and regulations. The dress worn by a debutante would traditionally be white or, by 1923, a light pastel and have a train attached to the shoulders. The debutante could carry flowers or a fan, and white gloves were required, as was a headdress made up of a tulle veil and white feathers and worn toward the left side of the head. (In previous decades, debutantes would have worn a single towering ostrich feather.)

Lady Rose's debutante dress was a bespoke creation, made by Kim Witcher and overseen by costume designer Caroline McCall. Its full skirt, created with the help of hip panniers, and close-fitting top are an example of robe de style, a signature look of French fashion designer Jeanne Lanvin. The style was briefly popular in the 1920s as an alternative to the straight-cut shift dress, and it seems appropriate that Rose would choose a dress at the height of its fashion. Its beautifully feminine and romantic silhouette, reminiscent of court dresses in the eighteenth century, suits Lady Rose and the occasion perfectly.

The pale pink silk dress, with a scooped neckline and a metallic lace overlay, is decorated with ribbon-work garlands of roses—in reference to her name, Lady Rose—and has a matching lace train. She also wears a diamond drop pendant necklace, cream evening gloves, and a headdress of ostrich feather plumes and soft tulle.

Lady Rose breezes into Downton Abbey as a young eighteen-year-old, ready to experience all the thrills of adulthood. While always stylish and elegant, her wardrobe reflected her youthfulness and fun-loving nature.

Rose is keen to find love, and we see her pursue various dalliances until she meets and falls in love with Atticus Aldridge, whom she marries. She moves to New York and becomes a mother, and over the series, we watch her shift to reflect the change from footloose party girl to sophisticated grown woman.

Rose never loses her effervescent energy, however, and Anna Robbins always wanted to ensure that Lily James, who plays Rose, could twirl around just as Rose would in costume with flair, energy, and movement. This was the thinking behind the blue coat Rose wore in season five, which had pleating all around to create a certain swish when Rose walked or spun around. Her silk knit dress of navy and pink displayed namesake roses, as we see in many of Rose's outfits throughout the series.

Following spread: Rose wears an original 1920s evening dress in seasons five and six, including when she visits Brancaster Castle and brings the gramophone out and has a dance. Bearing chevron patterning and namesake rose motifs, the beaded dress worked perfectly on Rose, both in its prettiness and its fashionable dropped waist and higher hemline. The vintage dress was in near-perfect condition, requiring just a little restoration.

During a visit to Downton Abbey with his parents, Atticus proposes to Rose and she excitedly accepts. Rose wears an original intricately beaded dress—with silver and white bugle beading on a pretty pink cotton base—along with a signature rose in her hair and palest pink silk gloves. The dress is slim-fitting down to hip level and then flares out, creating that sense of movement and fluidity often seen in Rose's wardrobe.

When it came to Lady Rose, the costume team was able to tap into a source of original dresses that perfectly suited Rose's personality but were otherwise too pretty or frivolous for the likes of Mary or Edith. It opened up a palette of pastel pinks and powder blues and especially feminine floral patterns and meant they could explore the popular and quintessential mid-1920s fashions that were more readily available through collectors and traders.

Anna Robbins: "Rose is feminine and has real warmth and a wonderful sense of fun. She loves going shopping and drinking cocktails, so we can have great fun with her style."

SPORTING AND OUTDOOR PURSUITS

HUNTING

The aristocracy is a sporting breed, and country pursuits—particularly in the form of hunting, shooting, and fishing—were integral to life on a large estate like Downton Abbey. A family like the Crawleys had the land and means to follow such activities, and the year revolved round a strict calendar of sporting events. King Edward VII held huge shooting parties at his estate in Sandringham, further boosting its popularity among the elite, although it was regarded as a men-only sport, with the ladies—bedecked in tweeds and furs—joining the guns for outdoor lunch or walking alongside the shooters and beaters.

Women were far more involved in hunting and horses in general—they were encouraged to ride, and it was one of the rare arenas where they could compete with men—and Lady Mary certainly enjoys the sense of freedom as she gallops around the countryside. Whichever sport men and women engaged in, there was a strict code of dress, and woe betide any weekend visitor to Downton Abbey if he or she didn't have the correct type of tweeds for an afternoon of game shooting or the proper riding habit for a day of hunting.

Before a hunt at Downton Abbey, we often see the elegantly dressed riders and excitable hounds assemble outside the great house, with Carson and the footmen serving drinks, usually port (known as stirrup cups). Lord Grantham is in his "hunting pinks," which consists of a scarlet Melton wool coat with black velvet collar and cuffs and three brass buttons. According to the hunting dress code, he can only wear a red jacket because the master of the hunt (who wears four brass buttons) has bestowed on him "the hunt button" in recognition of his years spent riding with the hunt, without which he would wear a black jacket. The hunt button also entitles him to wear mahogany-topped black leather riding boots, which he wears with cream cavalry twill (a tough wool) breeches, a cotton high-tipped collar and cravat, known as a stock, along with a black silk top hat (a squatter version than top hats worn on other occasions, like a wedding), leather gloves, and a gold stock pin.

When we first see Lady Mary in her riding habit, she is riding sidesaddle and is elegantly dressed in midnight blue. Women could wear only blue or black when hunting. She wears a long, black twill jacket with a split at the back so she can move when riding; jodhpurs topped with a long matching skirt with a slanted hem so it hangs horizontally on horseback; a high, white barrel-knot cravat (stock), a top hat with fine veiling to protect against mud splatters—only ladies riding sidesaddle could wear a top hat—and leather gloves. Ladies were also required to wear a corset when riding, although a little shorter than those worn with dresses, which some claim helped keep the rider stable when riding sidesaddle. While Michelle Dockery loved the look of her riding habit, she found the leather boots, which had lace and hooks running to above the knee, difficult to get on and off!

Lady Mary must wear either blue or black for the hunt, and Lord Grantham wears a scarlet-red hunting coat.

I n season five, Mary competes in a point-to-point, a form of racing in the countryside over fences, with the family and assembled guests, including Mary's suitor, Tony Gillingham, looking on. It's a physically demanding activity, but Mary prides herself on her horsemanship and is aware she looks sensational in her outfit, much to fellow competitor Mabel Lane Fox's annoyance (Mabel is trying to win over Tony): "Why turn up looking like a cross between a *Vogue* fashion plate and a case of dynamite?" Unlike Mabel, Mary is still riding sidesaddle (so as not to alarm her grandmother), and her green soft-checked wool riding habit comprises an ankle-length skirt with double-breasted short jacket, a cotton shirt with turndown collar, a brown silk tie, and a bowler. To create the ensemble, costume designer Anna Robbins had researched old Pathé films of female competitors at point-to-point races in the 1920s, who, with their full angled skirts and nipped-in waists, provided a great silhouette on horseback, a look she was keen to recreate for Mary.

Mary also wears a veiled brown bowler, the color of was discussed between costume designer Anna Robbins and *Downton*'s historical advisor Alastair Bruce. A brown bowler was better suited to the original leather boots Mary was wearing and to her brown leather gloves, but it was only when Anna could provide evidence that women at the time did sometimes wear brown hats, as opposed to the more usual black, that they agreed they could retain the brown version.

By the start of season six, Lady Mary is riding astride, and here she wears a fitted midnight-blue jacket with breeches and black bowler. Two versions of this outfit were required—one clean and one muddied—as Mary falls while jumping.

SHOOTING PARTY

Tweeds worn for country pursuits were an essential part of an aristocrat's wardrobe. They still have a timeless appeal in today's fashion, and *Downton Abbey* sparked a renewed interest in the look, with the likes of Ralph Lauren and Burberry featuring checked jackets and tweeds as part of their runway collections. Here, the men (opposite, Tom Branson in season five, and below, Matthew Crawley and Sir Richard Carlisle in season two) wear tweed suits in various greens, browns, and checks, plus four breeches, turndown collars, ties, and leather boots and gaiters. Tom's shooting suit, as featured on the mannequin (opposite), was made in Donegal tweed. The suit was also made with matching full-length trousers. Mary's checked tweed jacket and matching skirt were based on a suit belonging to real-life socialite Heather Firbank, although Mary's is a more fitted version.

Following spread: A shooting party from the season two Christmas special features, left to right, Lord Hepworth, Lady Rosamund, Lord Grantham, Sir Richard Carlisle, Lady Mary, and Matthew Crawley.

For the annual cricket match against the village, the props team provided period-style batting pads, bats, and balls, and a former cricketer advised on cricketing techniques of the time.

We have also seen the men of Downton Abbey, both upstairs and downstairs, engage in a game of cricket. Here, "whites" (sometimes called flannels) are worn, made up of a long-sleeved shirt, cable-knit V-necked woolen sweater, and trousers in either white or cream, and there is no distinction between lord or servant on the pitch. The ladies look on, dressed in cream-colored day dresses and hats, their parasols sheltering them from the sun. Set against the green pitch and cricket pavilion, it makes for a typically English scene.

TENNIS

The 1920s saw the emergence of "sportswear" for men and women, which loosely meant comfortable clothes for leisure as championed by French fashion designer Jean Patou and others. There was also a vogue for tennis in the period, popularized by French player Suzanne Lenglen, who was the darling of Wimbledon in the 1920s and wore Jean Patou–styled clothes. By the end of the 1920s, women were wearing knee-length, shift-like dresses, often with pleated skirts so they could move easily while playing tennis. In the second *Downton Abbey* movie, we see some of the characters dressed in tennis whites. Edith wears an original ivory silk dress, complete with little socks and low-heeled shoes, a simple barrette (slide) in her hair, and a wristwatch. Lucy wears an original silk dress in a squared weft pattern, the skirt gathered to add volume. She also wears a scarf in her hair and tortoiseshell glasses. The men wear long flannel trousers, Bertie in a shirt with rolled sleeves and original tank top and Tom in an original Aertex top. Both men are wearing belts, which was a very modern move for a gentleman of the period.

Tennis took off in the 1920s, as did the wearing of tennis whites. By the time of *A New Era*, skirt hemlines had risen, although men were still wearing long trousers.

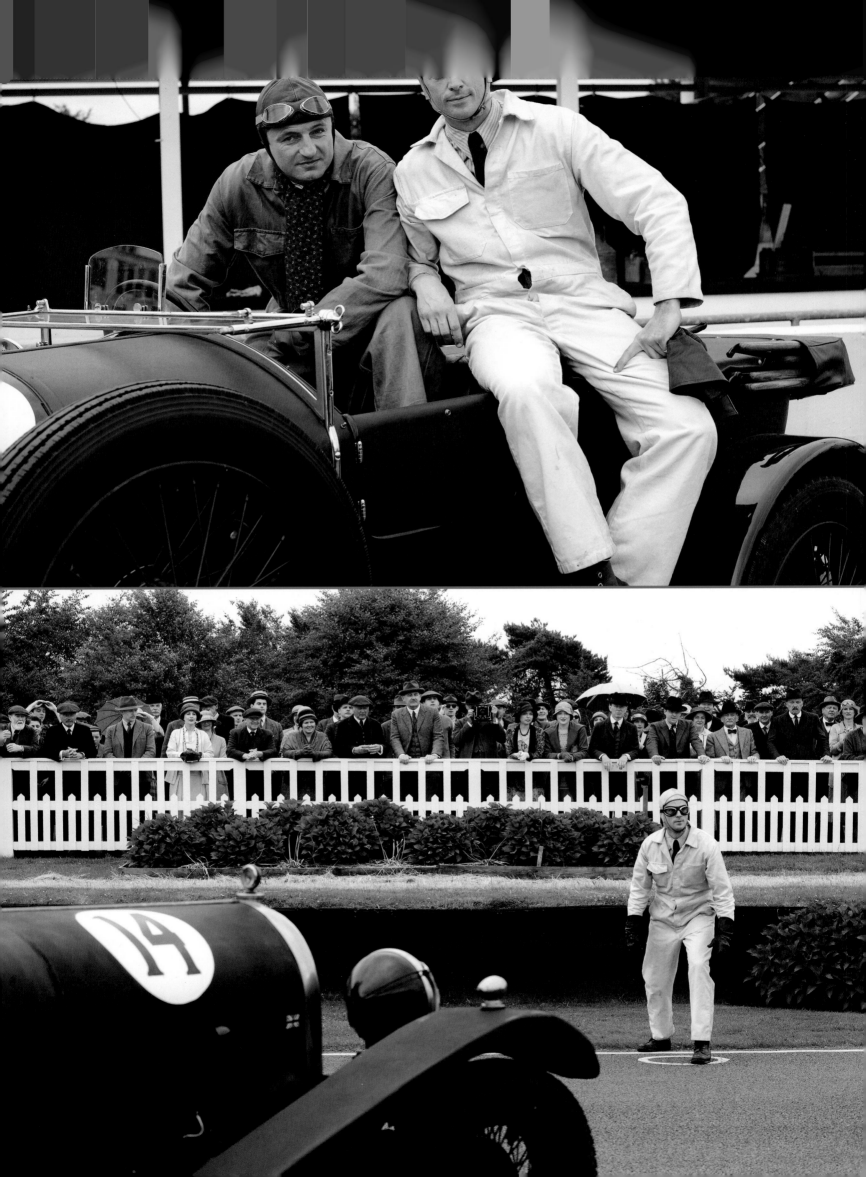

MOTORSPORT

T he likes of Henry Talbot are drawn to the new and exciting sport of car racing, and the aristocracy embraced the advent of the motorcar. When the Crawley family attend a race at Brooklands, the world's first purpose-built racing circuit, we see a variety of racing uniforms on participants who are still driving in open-topped cars and need protection from the elements. Henry wears heavy cotton coveralls over a shirt and tie, a leather cap and motoring goggles, and driving gloves. The day takes a tragic turn when Henry's friend Charles Rogers is killed in a fiery crash during the race.

In dressing Henry Talbot and all the drivers at Brooklands, the costume department looked at various historical images, including Sig Haugdahl (above right) and a female driver, both pioneers in the car racing world in the 1920s.

TOM BRANSON

om Branson is now a member of the Crawley family, having first arrived at Downton Abbey many years earlier as the family chauffeur. Moving from below stairs to above is an unusual change of circumstances, and there has been a gradual but noticeable change to his wardrobe over the years. Tom was born and raised in County Wicklow, Ireland, and when we first met him, he was dressed in the livery of a chauffeur, although it's soon apparent that he has hopes for a very different life.

Tom, or Branson as he is initially known to the family, first talks to Sybil while he is at the wheel of the family car. He is dressed in a heavy, double-breasted coat sporting double-breasted brass buttons, breeches, leather boots, large driving gloves, and a peaked cap with goggles resting on top. It is 1913, still very early days for automobiles, and most

were open to the weather, so like those of Downton Abbey's former coachmen, Tom's uniform needs to be warm and hard-wearing.

A relationship soon develops between Sybil and Tom—they are both idealistic and interested in politics, he in socialism and she in women's rights—and they eventually move away and marry. When the couple return to Downton, Tom is no longer in uniform but wears instead a brown Donegal tweed suit, which is more Irish working class in feel and fabric. Sybil tragically dies giving birth to their daughter, and Tom ends up living at Downton Abbey, which makes for an uneasy adjustment on both sides. United in their grief for Sybil, however, the family ultimately welcome Tom.

Tom warms to the Crawley family but often feels politically conflicted living among them, as Allen Leech, who plays Tom, explains: "Branson's always slightly baffled by the aristocracy and their ways and probably sees them in a similar way to the audience of *Downton.*" At first, Tom resists playing along with all the rules but soon realizes he must pick his battles, conceding that it's easier to wear black tie for dinner rather than have a discussion every evening about what he is wearing.

Taking on the role of estate manager at Downton, Tom is increasingly seen in suits, his look now country gentleman rather than working man. Throughout the series, the costume departments had his suits made in Donegal tweed as a nod to Branson's Irish heritage and as Tom himself would have chosen. He wore the oatmeal three-piece suit (see page 194) with plus fours, knee-length socks, brogues, and a brown felt homburg for shooting, and he also wore the jacket with full-length trousers when working on the Downton estate. A repeat of the suit was also made for the scene at the Brooklands racetrack in season six, as the costume department needed to dirty it down when Tom pulls Henry Talbot from a burning car.

Tom's look changes significantly during the series, from the uniform of a chauffeur to smart suits in Donegal tweeds.

By the time we reach the first *Downton Abbey* film, Tom is still wearing Donegal tweeds, but they are more obviously bespoke, as are his formal evening suits. "In the second film, there is no longer any difference in the way he and the Crawley men dress," explains Anna Robbins. "Branson is fully assimilated into the upper-class way of life, and the tweed of his suiting mirrors Robert's, although cut and styled to suit his character and age." In *A New Era*, set in the late 1920s, the costume department was able to explore some of the emerging trends for menswear like the double-breasted suit, which dispensed with the waistcoat. Branson is dressed in a pale-linen double-breasted suit in the South of France, which, without a waist-coat, is cooler for the Mediterranean heat and a fashionable take on holiday attire. He also dons fashionable tennis gear and swimwear, a look far removed from his chauffeur days.

Tom is dressed in formal white tie, complete with breeches, when the King and Queen come to stay at Downton Abbey in the first film.

LUCY SMITH

Lucy Smith, played by Tuppence Middleton, first arrives at Downton Abbey as a lady's maid to Lady Bagshaw, a distant relative of Lord Grantham. It is soon revealed that Lucy is the secret daughter of Lady Bagshaw. On meeting, Lucy and Tom Branson are instantly attracted to each other, and the second film begins with their joyous wedding and ends with the couple, amid the Crawley family, cradling their newborn baby.

Like Tom Branson, Lucy has experienced an unexpected rise in social status, which is reflected in her wardrobe. In the first movie, she is dressed smartly as a lady's maid and arrives wearing a gray-lilac coat with a navy blue silk dress underneath. To add interest, the costume team added hand-embroidered motifs down the center of the dress, and she wears original shoes and a little cloche, looking very on trend for the 1920s.

By the second movie, she is now heir to the Bagshaw estate and a member of the aristocracy. Lucy joins the Crawley party heading to the French Riviera, and there we see her in a variety of summery outfits that work well in the sunshine of the Mediterranean. "Lucy is able to express herself through clothing in a way she never has before," explains Anna Robbins, "so she has fun with it. There's a prettiness and lightheartedness to the way she dresses, but it's not frivolous or over the top."

In *A New Era,* we see Lucy dressed in an original white dress made of cotton tulle with beautiful embroidery, with a dropped waist and shirring to gather a fuller skirt. "We matched the ivory color and mirrored the lovely U-shape neckline in a slip for her to wear underneath," explains Anna, "but it sits just in on the sleeve and neckline, allowing the lace to play against the skin. The whole effect was rather dreamy and lovely, and she wore some fabulous original tortoiseshell sunglasses with it as well.

"The yellow dress [see page 205] is an original printed chiffon two-piece comprising belted dress with soft cowl neckline and matching jacket. It's beautifully lightweight and has a sunshiny 1930s feel to it."

Lucy Smith looks smart as a lady's maid, and then we see her in a variety of pretty, summery outfits in the South of France.

WEDDINGS

MARY AND MATTHEW

The weddings of *Downton Abbey* always cause something of a stir, both within the fictional household of the Crawleys and with the millions of viewers who tune in to catch a glimpse of *the dress*. The influence of *Downton*'s costumes—known as "the Downton effect"—has permeated fashion across the globe, but the spotlight often falls most on the wedding gowns. *Downton* weddings make for happy and stunning spectacles, which in turn have influenced bridal fashion today, with couples keen to incorporate elements of the early twentieth century into their nuptials, whether it's a 1920s-style headpiece or a vintage-inspired lace dress.

The first wedding featured in the series was that of Lady Mary and Matthew Crawley. The previous two seasons had followed their will they–won't they romance (compounded by Matthew's betrothal to Lavinia Swire), so *Downton* fans and the Crawleys breathed a huge sigh of relief when they finally exchanged vows. Lady Edith also walks down the aisle in the same season, so costume designer Caroline McCall had the task of creating two wedding dresses for the sisters. Having researched weddings of the early 1920s, Caroline knew that there were two dominant fabrics for bridal gowns, lace and satin, and she chose lace for Mary and a design inspired by that of Jeanne Lanvin, a French fashion house of the period.

The dress, made by Jane Law, consisted of palest apricot chiffon with lace tabard overlay and a slightly dropped-waist sash. Mary's dress has a romantic medieval look that was very fashionable in the early 1920s. She also wears a tulle veil and platinum-and-diamond tiara, which would have been a family heirloom. In reality, the tiara dates to the Georgian era and was loaned to the costume department by the famous London jewelers Bentley & Skinner. "While this is a traditional tiara," explains Caroline, "Lady Mary is very fashionable, so I felt strongly that she should wear it in a fashionable way. Bentley & Skinner allowed us to take it off its frame so Mary could wear it lower on her forehead."

Costume designers also play close attention to the script, and Caroline knew that the first time we see Mary's dress was when she walked down the flower-adorned stairs of Downton's great hall, with light falling on her. "I really wanted her to shimmer," says Caroline, "so the lace of her dress had some metallic thread running through it." The general effect of her gown is, of course, stunning, and Lord Grantham and Mr. Carson are captivated when she first appears on the stairs. Mary asks in her typically nonchalant way, "Will I do, Carson?" To which he answers, "Very nicely, my lady."

A short while after Mary's wedding, Edith walks down the aisle looking equally lovely in a full-length satin dress and embroidered train. It has a similar silhouette to Lady Mary's dress and is very much of the period, with hip gathers, long chiffon sleeves, a tulle veil, and the same platinum-and-diamond tiara, a family heirloom, that Lady Mary wore to her wedding.

Sadly for Edith, the day doesn't go as planned, as her considerably older groom, Sir Anthony Strallan, decides at the last minute not to go ahead with the wedding and leaves Edith stranded at the altar. Back at Downton, Edith is humiliated and flings her floor-length veil over the banisters. While it's an unfortunate occurrence for poor Edith, she has at least escaped becoming "an old man's drudge" as her grandmother Violet feared might be her fate.

The inspiration for Edith's dress, which was made by Jane Law, came from its train. It was originally part of a court presentation dress, which had been purchased by Downton Abbey's milliner Sean Barrett. "He had shown me the train the year before," explains Caroline McCall, "and I remembered it because it had exquisite beading and embroidery. So I asked if I could borrow it and decided to design Edith's dress around the train, using satin crepe for the dress and picking up elements of the embroidery on the side of it."

Caroline McCall: "We wanted Edith's dress to be fairly simple and in a 1920s-style fabric that draped well on her figure. Edwardian fabrics tended to be much heavier."

ANNA AND MR. BATES

Season two sees four members of the downstairs staff marry, although both ceremonies are hurriedly arranged, so the brides and grooms must spruce up whatever they have in their wardrobe. The first wedding we see is that of former footman William, who has been severely wounded fighting in the war, to kitchen maid Daisy. William lies in bed, gravely ill, while the vicar conducts the ceremony. With swags of flower garlands decorating the bed frame, it makes for a particularly poignant scene, with even Violet reaching for the tissues. Daisy has her hair in a pretty style, adorned with a yellow flower, and wears a blouse in a floral pattern and a floor-length skirt. William tragically dies just a few hours later.

Later on in the season, head housemaid Anna and valet Mr. Bates tie the knot in an unassuming but touching wedding ceremony at the Ripon Register Office. They also exchange their vows in something of a rush, just days before Bates is sent to prison after he is wrongly accused of his ex-wife's murder. The pair don their Sunday best, with Anna in a simple white cotton blouse and blue ribboned hat and Bates in his best three-piece suit with matching tie.

While the weddings of the staff downstairs are less lavish affairs, they make for particularly poignant moments in Downton Abbey.

When Lady Rose married Atticus Aldridge, Anna Robbins had the opportunity to design two wedding outfits: the first for the register office ceremony (Atticus is Jewish, so they cannot marry in a church) and a second, more formal gown for the reception afterward. For the register office, Anna made a blue crepe silk dress for Rose, with a dropped waist and matching jacket, much of which was designed around a vintage collar and trim she had come across in a Parisian vintage shop months before. "We didn't want bridal white for Rose, and this soft powder-blue color felt pretty and right for her." She also wears a hat adorned with her namesake roses (real and preserved), its wide brim allowing light to filter through and mirroring her pretty collar: "I wanted this outfit to show Rose had blossomed from a young girl into a grown woman," explains Anna, "without losing her sense of fun or effervescence."

At the reception, Rose wears an original sequined tulle dress that Anna had discovered in Pennies Vintage, a shop in Islington, which she accessorized with cream gloves and a delicate seed pearl headdress, with clusters of real roses set into the waves of her hair. "The gown was boxed and, with its fastenings unfinished, had clearly never been worn," Anna says. "But as soon as I saw it, I knew it was perfect for Rose. It had an empire line, so was probably from a little earlier than the 1920s, but it was so pretty and utterly romantic, which made it quintessentially Rose. With dainty sequins in cream, oyster, and rose gold and a sweeping circular train, the dress was perfection. We knew it was fragile, and even with some careful conservation, the dress didn't fare well during the two days of filming, with the tulle starting to pull apart under the weight of being worn. That broke my heart a bit, but then I took comfort from the fact that a dress that was very possibly owned by a wartime widow and never saw its happily ever after got that moment, in such a special way, on film, preserved now forever."

For her wedding reception, Rose appears in an original, never-before-worn beaded dress of silk tulle over an ivory and buttery silk underdress that complemented her skin tone. Her stunning headdress is made out of preserved roses, which were also used in her bouquet.

For the joyful occasion of Mrs. Hughes and Mr. Carson's wedding, Mrs. Patmore and Miss Baxter had to persuade the Downton housekeeper to wear something a little more ornate than her simple gray dress. In the end, after a little misunderstanding, Lady Grantham donates one of her coats, which Baxter then alters by removing its original fur collar and hem to suit Mrs. Hughes.

In reality, the costume team made the coat for the scene, their aim to create something that would believably belong in Cora's wardrobe but would also suit Mrs. Hughes and the occasion. To that end, they made a beautiful velvet coat in a mauve typical of Cora's palette, onto which they appliquéd original 1920s lace, embellished with silk flowers, velvet leaves, and clusters of pearl beads, all handworked and taking over 150 hours to complete. Nonetheless, Anna Robbins took real pleasure in designing a wedding outfit for a downstairs character and dressing her in a bit of upstairs finery. Mrs. Hughes also wears a gray, wide-brimmed straw hat with matching fabric floral decoration, with the suggestion that Miss Baxter may have added some decoration to spruce up an otherwise simple hat. Carson wears his Sunday best, a blue-gray three-piece tweed suit with a navy silk tie and a black felt bowler hat.

Mrs. Hughes wears a beautiful velvet coat for her wedding to Mr. Carson. In the storyline, the coat originally belonged to Cora and had a vintage fur collar that Miss Baxter removed to suit Mrs. Hughes better.

W hen Lady Mary marries Henry Talbot—her former husband, Matthew Crawley, having been tragically killed four years earlier—she opts for a smaller wedding. She's already had the big lavish do, and this simpler version proves just as moving, as we can see that Mary has finally given her heart to another and can move on with her life. The wedding also is hastily arranged, and Anna Robbins's challenge was to create an outfit that was bridal in look but suited the pared-down occasion. The result was a cream textured elegant matka silk dress with a knife-pleat skirt and an exaggerated dropped waist, which was very on trend for 1925. Over the dress she wears a matching jacket with vintage lace trim insertions, accessorized with a single string of pearls. The ivory straw hat she wears is adorned with ribbon, tulle, and butterflies, the latter representative of new beginnings and a fresh start for Mary, with the handsome and debonair Henry Talbot by her side.

Anna Robbins: "I wanted the outfit Lady Mary wore for her marriage to Henry Talbot to be simple yet chic. Henry wears a formal morning suit with pale dove-gray waistcoat and a stiff turndown rather than wing-tipped collar for a modern edge."

Lady Edith finally finds happiness when she and Bertie Pelham fall in love, their wedding taking place in the last television episode of *Downton Abbey*. It is a lavish affair, as befitting of a marquess and an earl's daughter, followed by a large reception back at Downton, which coincides with New Year's celebrations, the clock at midnight chiming in 1926.

Edith's wedding dress also represented something of a high point for Anna Robbins and her team, who were determined to create something very special for Edith. When working on a period drama, Anna regularly trawls through vintage photographs and is often especially captivated by bridal images from the 1920s: "They have this unusual, ethereal feel about them, a moment in time captured in sepia, with lots of frothy layers of tulle and lace, and I was keen to encapsulate a sense of that with Edith's dress."

The starting point for Edith's dress came in the form of an original ivory lace dress that Anna found at the same shop where she sourced Rose's wedding dress. It was made of exquisite two-tiered Brussels lace, but its neckline and sleeves weren't quite right and needed elevating: "My plan was to graft a different lace onto the top of the dress to create a softer, more beautiful neckline, onto the bottom to add length, and to replace the sleeves. So I went on this lace-finding exploration over the course of a few months, during which I stumbled upon the most remarkable train made of Brussels lace, which looked like it had been made for the dress. So that was a happy addition to the dress and it sweeps behind Edith as she walks down the aisle. The dress itself tapered down to the finest lace layer, which looked really beautiful when Edith was standing, backlit by the slanting rays of sunlight through the church windows."

Edith also wears a seed pearl tiara, markedly and consciously different from the one she wore on her first ill-fated wedding day. At her reception, she swaps her tiara for a pearl headdress worn low on her forehead with an asymmetric draped tassel, which is a particularly 1920s look, highlighting that Edith is very much a modern woman who knows her own style and place in the world.

Edith's wedding dress is ankle-length, tapering down to the finest lace layer, which works beautifully against her skin and in church light.

A *New Era* opens with Tom Branson's wedding to Lucy Smith, a summery, joyful event and very much a friendly, family affair. With that in mind, Anna Robbins wanted to create a wedding dress for Lucy that was fashion-forward and on trend for the period but fresh and relaxed at the same time: "I wanted us to feel Lucy could gather up her skirts and really dance at her wedding reception. So it had to be beautiful, of course, but also joyful and lighthearted.

"I loved the idea of layers and layers of silk tulle spraying out from a low-waisted bodice, so we created a dress made up of ivory satin and chiffon with a boatneck, long sleeves, and layers and layers of stiffened silk tulle for the skirts, which were cut higher at the front and into a train at the back—very on point for 1928. The resulting silhouette is dramatic but has a weightless frothiness to it.

"For the satin bodice, we mounted antique silver-thread embroidered net onto the satin, and for Lucy's veil, we sourced a hand-embroidered replica of a 1920s original. The bodice had a low back, which is quite daring, but I wanted it to have impact because the first shot of the film sees Tom and Lucy standing at the altar with their backs to us."

Lucy also wears an original diamond bow brooch just below her collarbone and an original diamond-and-pearl tiara for the ceremony, which she swaps for a diamanté and quintessentially 1920s-style Juliet cap at the reception.

Lucy's wedding dress was inspired by various bridal images from the 1920s, including this image of Edwina Erwin in 1920s. Tuppence Middleton, who plays Lucy, had four costume fittings for the wedding dress, a luxury for the costume team, who normally have to make do with only one or two fittings for each outfit. But everyone tends to make an exception for bridal wear.

BELOW
STAIRS

MR. CARSON

Mr. Carson, the long-serving and now-retired butler of Downton Abbey, has always been loyal to the Crawley family. As the most senior figure of the servant household, he takes great pride in his role and insists on the highest standards. Dignity is his watchword, and while he can be a very upright and stern figure, there is a gentleness to his character; he has always had a soft spot for Lady Mary, and shows fatherly concern for the servants of the house. He is sometimes bewildered by the rapidly changing world and hankers for the past, when everyone knew their place.

In the main, we see Mr. Carson, played by Jim Carter, in his butler's uniform, both evening and day versions. Unlike the footmen, he is not liveried but wears clothing that is similar in look to the gentlemen of the house. Mr. Carson always ensures he is impeccably turned out and expects the same of his footmen, who are given a strong ticking off if they are not correctly attired. His day uniform consists of formal day dress: a black wool morning coat and waistcoat worn with morning trousers, in this case, gray-and-black-striped wool trousers. He also wears a white cotton shirt, stiff imperial collar, and black wool tie, and he always accessorizes his day uniform with a silver Double Albert pocket watch worn across both waistcoat pockets. There is a rigid structure to every day: Servants must be up early preparing for the day, and Mr. Carson must keep a careful eye on the time. However, unlike Lord Grantham, he never replaced his pocket watch with a wristwatch.

For evening service, Mr. Carson changes into formal white tie, which also consists of a stiff white collar and starched shirt. Mr. Carson's uniform has remained unchanged over the series and films, with bespoke tailoring by Cosprop and, in later years, by Chris Kerr. Bespoke tailoring has a number of advantages, not least that it can help actors get into

character, as Susannah Buxton remembers with Mr. Carson's uniform: "It is extraordinary what a bespoke suit can do to a person's shape. Jim is a big bear of a man, and the tailoring helped him stand taller, and he also felt psychologically more upright when he wore it. "Jim has also quipped that in real life he dresses formally "only under duress," and, in fact, the only time Mr. Carson has worn clothing similar to the type Jim might wear himself was when we see Carson in cricket whites, as Jim is a lifelong fan of cricket.

Mr. Carson wears a daytime uniform consisting of a three-piece morning suit before changing into formal white tie for evening service.

When Mr. Carson retires, we see him out of uniform, generally in a three-piece tweed suit and tie. He looks smart but somehow not himself, and we sense he's itching to get back into the tailcoat and high collars. Whatever Carson wears, he always has a pocket watch tucked into his waistcoat, and if it's very hot outside, he might replace his bowler hat with a fedora. When he travels to the French Riviera in *A New Era*, he insists on wearing his full butler uniform and usual tweed suit despite the Mediterranean heat. Having never been abroad and a little suspicious of foreigners, he's determined to look the part of an Englishman, but, of course, simply gets hot and bothered in the process.

Mr. Carson always likes to look smart, even when he is not in a butler's livery. He favors a bowler hat and is accustomed to dressing for the cooler climes of Yorkshire.

MRS. HUGHES

Mrs. Hughes runs the household on behalf of Lady Grantham, ensuring the entire house is spick-and-span, the beds are made, and the family and their guests are well looked after. It's a weighty responsibility, and Mrs. Hughes is efficient, thoroughly experienced, and, like Mr. Carson, has high standards. The pair eventually marry, and her more liberal outlook acts as a good foil to Mr. Carson's more conservative tendencies. She can also be counted on to provide solid moral counsel to the staff within her charge.

Working from early morning to night, Mrs. Hughes is invariably dressed in uniform, which consists of black or dark-colored bodices, high necks, and long skirts. While in uniform, she retains the corseted Edwardian silhouette, with a belted waist and hair neatly tied back, although in later seasons, she adopts a more relaxed silhouette in her civilian wear, albeit modestly so. Her clothing is practical but considered and well fitted. She wears a separate day and evening uniform, her day uniform a little plainer, although the costume department always added some texture or embellishment to give a bit of interest on-screen. Her evening uniform has a little more sheen to it, with the use of silk, velvet, or more intricate embroidery. In the uniform (right and opposite), she wears a black damask wool bodice and a patterned lace inbuilt infill with jet buttons, with an appliqué-trim velvet belt and cuffs and long matching skirt with gathered back.

Mrs. Hughes is always seen with a series of chains (known as a chatelaine) hanging off her belt, on which are attached household keys and a pair of scissors. In a large house like Downton Abbey, everything from the linen and writing desks to food cupboards and spices had to be locked up, and only the housekeeper or mistress to the house had access to them. Just as Mr. Carson is rarely seen without his pocket watch, such is the case with Mrs. Hughes's chatelaine, the swish of her long skirts and the jangle of her keys no doubt a common sound in the corridors of Downton Abbey.

Mrs. Hughes is rarely out of her uniform, and when she is, she is often in her Sunday best, consisting of a fitted blue jacket and long skirt, belted in at the waist, with perhaps a pretty scarf and a hat adorned with a ribbon and flower. She has an eye for detail and is always well turned out. When she and the other servants visited the seaside in season four, it was a delight to see her in more relaxed clothing, her jacket removed, blouse loose, and her skirts gathered up in her hands so she can paddle in the lapping waters.

Mrs. Hughes wore this evening uniform throughout seasons three and four. So that it would perfectly fit Phyllis Logan, who plays Mrs. Hughes, it was made in-house by the costume department.

MRS. PATMORE

There has been little change to the look of Mrs. Patmore, Downton Abbey's cook. She is a busy woman with multiple meals to prepare every day, and she has little time to fuss over her clothes. Her uniform is the same day and night, consisting of a matching printed cotton blouse and long, gathered skirt, linen apron with pockets, and cotton cap, although she always has a clean pressed apron on standby so she can look presentable if she is summoned upstairs.

While the general silhouette of Mrs. Patmore's uniform has largely remained the same, colors and fabric patterns have varied over the seasons from a fawn leaf-printed pattern to lilac and a soft turquoise, which go well with Lesley Nicol's red hair.

When not working, Mrs. Patmore dons a dark-colored jacket and long skirt, a suit that has served her well over the years. Other than varying the blouses underneath or dispensing with the jacket if it's a summer day, she wears this suit invariably. She may have replaced the odd button or repaired its simple frogging—Mrs. Patmore is nothing if not practical—and she'll probably continue wearing it for a few years to come.

Mrs. Patmore's uniform is practical and comfortable, and was made specially for Lesley Nicol, who plays the Downton cook. Her linen bib-fronted apron with deep pockets is essential when preparing food in the kitchen.

DAISY

Daisy is first employed at Downton Abbey as a kitchen maid assisting the cook, Mrs. Patmore, as well as taking on general household duties, which include cleaning and lighting the fireplaces every day. It is dirty work, and for that reason, she must keep out of the way of the family upstairs. Her uniform is less formal than the housemaids', and she wouldn't be expected to change it in the evening. When she first arrives at Downton Abbey, she is young and impressionable, given to romantic crushes, and at the beck and call of an often irritable Mrs. Patmore, although the two develop a close bond.

In the first season, Daisy wears a pink ankle-length dress with a practical cotton apron tied around her waist to protect her dress. Unlike many of the downstairs uniforms, which were either hired from costumiers or made in-house by the costume team, this was an original maid's dress. "It's quite rare to find an original servant piece like this," explains Susannah Buxton, who found the dress. "The cotton has this wonderful papery quality to it and it suited Daisy really well."

By seasons three and four, Daisy has been promoted to assistant cook and wears a more formal kitchen uniform, similar to the clothing worn by Mrs. Patmore. It consists of a long-sleeved cotton dress in fine gray pinstripe, a cream linen apron with a bib front, and a cap and was made in-house by the costume team.

Along with taking on more responsibility downstairs, Daisy catches up with the education she missed as a girl and grows in confidence. As a result, she starts to form her own opinions about the world and question her future.

Over the course of *Downton Abbey* we watch Daisy mature from a timid, scatter-brained kitchen maid to a more assertive woman in her twenties, and her costume and look reflect that growth. When not in uniform, she would have worn the few civilian clothes she had on multiple occasions. Clothing and fabric were expensive, and a servant's salary did not extend to an extensive wardrobe. For that reason, the costume team usually hired Daisy's off-duty clothing from costumers, as they did for other servants. "The hire houses have a great range of everyday separates," explains Anna Robbins, "which, to our advantage, have a bit of softness and wear to them. Daisy's wardrobe would be made up of clothing that she wears often and that has to last years, only to be replaced when unrepairable or worn through. It's important to read that in the fabric of the clothing she wears."

Like any young woman, Daisy is interested in fashion and has her hair cut into a stylish bob. She is also thrilled when Hollywood stars descend on Downton in *A New Era* and takes great delight in their dazzling looks. By now she is married to Andy, a footman, and seems more content with her life, although she no doubt has great plans for their future together.

Daisy eventually marries Andy, the footman, and we increasingly see her out of her housemaid's uniform and in her own clothes.

HOUSEMAIDS

The housemaids at Downton Abbey wear a daytime uniform for their long list of household chores and a smarter evening uniform for later in the day or formal events. While there is far less variety downstairs when it comes to clothing, the servants' uniforms do subtly reflect the changing fashions—hemlines inch up, and small changes are made to aprons and headdresses.

Susannah Buxton, who established the look of all the characters in season one, wanted to create a uniformity for the downstairs characters, with green the dominant color in both the housemaids' day dresses and in the footmen's waistcoats. The maids' daytime dresses were made by the costume department in cotton with a green-and-navy weave print and were worn with linen aprons and caps. In reality, girls who entered service in this period would be required to make their own uniforms, sometimes out of a length of fabric given to them by their employers.

The evening uniform consisted of a black dress made from cotton sateen worn with a fine cotton apron. Early on in the series, the housemaids wore original Edwardian aprons, few of which have survived. For that reason, Susannah Buxton was thrilled to come across some when she was looking through garments at the costumier Cosprop. "On a dusty high shelf I came across a box and inside was a set of Edwardian broderie anglaise aprons," she says. "I almost jumped off the ladder for joy because they were totally right for the period and handmade in beautiful broderie anglaise, which we could have never reproduced ourselves."

THOMAS BARROW

W e've seen Thomas Barrow climb the ranks at Downton Abbey, from first footman to valet to under-butler, and finally, when Mr. Carson retires, he takes on the senior role of butler. He takes pride in his various uniforms and always looks sharp and well turned out.

In his younger years, he could be ruthlessly ambitious and cruel to anyone who got in his way. Gradually, however, we've seen a more vulnerable side to Thomas, particularly when we've witnessed his extreme anguish over his homosexuality, which caused him to try to take his own life.

Thomas also fought in the trenches of the First World War, and in a desperate attempt to be sent home, he purposely got shot in the hand, and thereafter wears a glove on one hand to hide the bullet wound.

Thomas has devoted much of his adult life to service—and there's not much he doesn't know about running a house like Downton Abbey—but when a romantic encounter with film star Guy Dexter leads to the opportunity to get away, he jumps at the chance. As dresser to a Hollywood star, he'll no longer need the starched white collars and tails, but he'll no doubt look just as sharp in whatever he wears.

Thomas is dressed as an underbutler (opposite). In the later *Downton* movies he wears the white-tie evening uniform of Downton's head butler (below).

FOOTMEN

Early on in the series, while serving the family at dinner, Mr. Carson spots a tear at the shoulder of William's tailcoat. It is an unacceptable transgression that must never happen again, he warns William: "You must remember a good servant at all times retains a sense of pride and dignity that reflects the pride and dignity of the family he serves." Mr. Carson knows better than anyone that footmen are regarded as showpieces of a great house. They are on public show upstairs and are usually dressed in opulent livery provided by their employers.

At Downton Abbey, the footmen wear a uniform that is not unlike the white-tie suits worn by the gentlemen of the house. They wear black wool tailcoats with brass livery buttons over matching formal trousers and striped waistcoats in sage and dark green, in a tone similar to the green day dresses of the housemaids. Under their waistcoats, they wear starched front piqué cotton shirts with stiff imperial wing collars and white piqué bowties, accessorized with gold and mother-of-pearl dress studs and gold oval cuff links. The whole attire, particularly the stiff collars and shirts that are "starched like cast iron," can feel uncomfortable for the actors who wear it, but it certainly makes them stand straighter, as Ed Speleers, who plays the footman Jimmy, put it: "The moment you put on those tails, the penguin suit, and the stiff collar, you start to feel yourself."

When not upstairs attending to the family or the guests, footmen have a range of household duties, from brushing and cleaning shoes and clothes to polishing brass and mirrors. For this dirtier work, they'll take off their smart tailcoat and wear a sleeved waistcoat to protect their shirt sleeves, often also putting on an apron and cuff protectors.

Left: Footman William Mason dispatches some simple darning. When downstairs, he takes off his long tailcoat.

When King George V and Queen Mary came to stay at Downton Abbey in *A New Era*, the footmen of the household—Andy, Albert, and Mr. Molesley (who is now a school teacher but chooses to return to help out)—replaced their usual footman attire for a more ornate style of livery. Great houses at the time would have kept dress livery for special occasions or for very grand guests—and there are none grander than the King and Queen. This provided a great opportunity for the costume department to design new uniforms for the downstairs staff.

Anna Robbins researched the type of livery they might have worn and set about making bespoke suits, with the help of *Downton*'s tailor Chris Kerr and specialist embroiderers Hand & Lock. Anna maintained the Downton uniform signature green, picking a dark rifle green that juxtaposed well with the scarlet livery of the royal household. The doeskin wool tailcoats were embellished with silver lacing and frogging detail on the body, sleeves, and pockets. The brass buttons were also stamped with the Crawley family's coat of arms, as designed by *Downton*'s historical advisor Alastair Bruce.

"Intricate work is put into making the tailcoats, to design the proportion of the tailcoat and the placement of its embellishment," explains Anna Robbins. "The silver lacing, made up of metallic flat ribbon work, was stitched down along the seams and box pleats of the coat. The frogging on the front of the coat was stitched with soutache, or Russia braid. The new tailcoats were paired with green velvet, laced waistcoats worn with a winged collar and piqué bow ties, white moleskin breeches, and white silk stockings and buckled patent pumps."

Once the suits were made, they were sent to the breakdown department to age them a little, so they didn't look brand new.

Laura Gunning, from the breakdown department, paints a subtle patina of age onto the silver detailing (top right). The Crawley family coat of arms (bottom right) was stamped on the brass buttons, which were made by *Downton*'s model maker, Martin Adams.

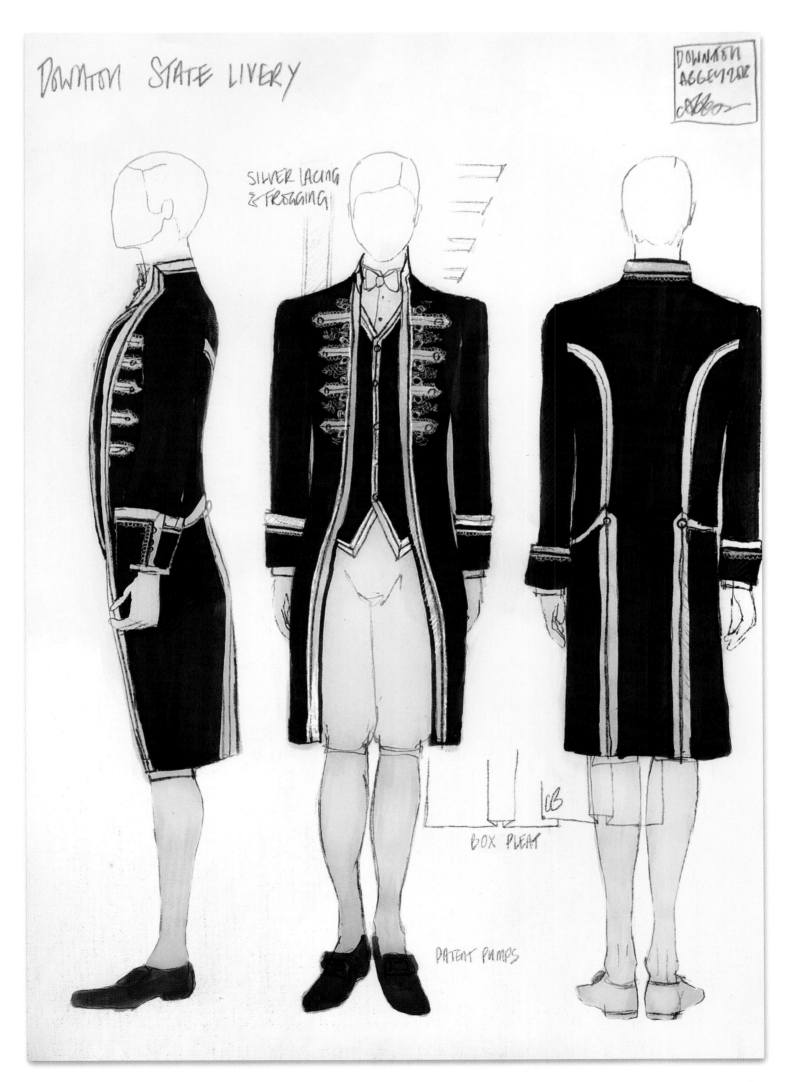

DOWNTON STATE LIVERY

SILVER LACING
& FROGGING

BOX PLEAT

PATENT PUMPS

ANNA

Former head housemaid Anna is now lady's maid to Mary and one of the more senior servants of the Downton Abbey household. Married to Mr. Bates and now a mother, Anna has suffered considerable misfortune over the years, from being sexually attacked by a visitor to the house to being falsely accused of murder. Throughout it all, she has remained morally upright, a steadfast and loving wife and mother, and a loyal servant and confidante to Lady Mary. She is often neat and tidy in appearance, wearing the usual black silk uniform of a lady's maid, which by season three has a dropped waistline and looser fit, in accordance with the changing styles in fashion.

Anna is interested in fashion—she'll happily flip through a magazine—and, as a lady's maid, it is her job to keep abreast of the latest trends so she can dress and advise Lady Mary accordingly. Her role involves not only dressing and undressing Mary but also brushing and styling her hair, while also maintaining her mistress's clothes, hats, and accessories. She must polish shoes and boots as well, a job she often does alongside Mr. Bates in the boot room. Lady's maids were also required to have dressmaking and millinery skills so they could repair and adapt clothes for both their mistresses and themselves.

With a daytime and evening uniform, Anna is always expected to be smartly dressed, especially if she is traveling with Lady Mary. When designing for Anna, who is played by Joanne Froggatt and whose clothes are always made by the costume team, Anna Robbins regularly added a little interest to the black silk of her uniform. In season five, her daytime dress has a tiny diamond jacquard pattern, along with twin-stitching detail that mirrors the angle of the diamonds. It's very neat and delicate and very Anna.

These little details are important because they are picked up on camera, even more so when *Downton Abbey* appears on the big screen. For the first movie, Anna Robbins redesigned Anna's evening uniform in a slightly glossier black silk. It is made up of a long waistcoat over a dress that has a floral pattern to it in a pretty but subtle way. By fastening at the low hip at the center, it's on trend, but it still has a classic and refined look, as is befitting for a lady's maid.

Anna was a housemaid when she first met Mr. Bates. Since then, she has progressed to lady's maid and is one of the more senior members of the household staff.

The servants at Downton Abbey would have had few civilian items of clothing, although the perk of being a lady's maid is that she could have the castoffs of her mistress. Anna is occasionally seen in items of clothing that were once worn by Lady Mary, and she would have had the dressmaking skills to alter any pieces that came her way.

In season two, Mary wears a striped blue dress and apron while attending to Matthew, who has been injured in the war. By the next season, Anna wears the same dress at the village cricket match, paired with a hat she no doubt spruced up, and she and Mr. Bates look an elegant couple.

For the Brooklands set piece in season six (below), Anna Robbins costumed Anna in a pretty cream silk blouse and wool skirt, dressed up with an almond pink 1920s coat with delicate chevron pin tuck detailing. Anna wore a brown crin hat with an upturned brim and decorative silk flowers that lent a lovely summery feeling to the ensemble. These individual pieces from Anna's wardrobe will have been reworn in other configurations across the series.

Anna always dresses smartly, even when she's not wearing the uniform of a lady's maid.

"I always enjoyed creating costumes for Anna; Joanne's frame is perfect for the 1920s and we both gravitate towards the same delicate detailing that suits Anna's kind, gentle manner and her professionalism as a lady's maid."

—ANNA ROBBINS

MR. BATES

r. Bates's clothing has changed very little during the years of *Downton Abbey*. From the first season, he has worn the standard valet attire, which is the same for both day and evening. It consists of a heavy wool twill single-breasted jacket and waistcoat worn with striped morning trousers, white cotton shirt with double round collar, and black wool tie. He also wears gold cuff links and a gold watch chain with pocket watch.

Like the character he played, Brendan Coyle was always mindful of the little details in his look, ensuring that he had the right watch chain, overcoat, and bowler hat, which became something of a signature piece for Mr. Bates. As a valet, it was Bates's job to attend to Lord Grantham's wardrobe, to select clothing for him, dress him, and keep his clothes in good order when needed. Duties involved cleaning his master's boots and shoes, brushing or cleaning items of clothing, packing sufficient clothing for a trip away, as well as generally being on hand when his master needed to change clothes during the day.

As a result, we usually see Mr. Bates in his valet uniform, with cane in hand due to a leg injury suffered during the Boer War. It's a rare day we see him in his shirtsleeves, as we do when he visits the seaside with the other servants. When he is accused of murder and is imprisoned, we see him in prison uniform, a rough gray wool jacket with stand collar over a waistcoat and collarless shirt.

Mr. Bates wears his valet uniform with pride and knows he is lucky to have retained his position after suffering a leg injury during the Boer War.

MR. MOLESLEY

Mr. Molesley has worked in various roles for the Crawley family, first as a butler to Matthew and Isobel Crawley in the village, then as valet and footman at Downton Abbey, before taking on the position of teacher at the local school. He often returned to work at Downton Abbey for special events or when the Crawley family were hosting large parties of guests. When the King and Queen come to stay, he considers it an honor to "slip on the livery again," although this time he must wear splendid dress livery. He's even more excited when Hollywood stars descend on Downton Abbey for *A New Era*.

Life has not been easy for Mr. Molesley: When Matthew died, he lost his valet job and had to work as a delivery boy and road mender before returning to Downton as a footman. He is clearly intelligent, and we sense his frustration with his lot in life. His luck turns, however, when he becomes a teacher at the village school and is then, having proved his talents, taken on as scriptwriter by Hollywood director Jack Barber, leading him then to propose to Miss Baxter.

Given his varied work history, we've therefore seen Mr. Molesley in a variety of clothing, from the uniforms of a butler, valet, and footman to civilian attire and the typical three-piece suit of a teacher. Now that he's landed his dream job as a scriptwriter, he'll more likely wear the casual separates and suits worn by film crews rather than the tails and stiff collars of a footman.

When working as a teacher, Mr. Molesley wears a three-piece suit, but he often slips on the livery of a footman when helping out at Downton Abbey.

MISS BAXTER

Miss Baxter, lady's maid to Cora, is a calm and kind presence downstairs who develops a close bond with Mr. Molesley. After her arrival at Downton, it's soon revealed that she has a checkered past, having served time in prison for stealing jewelry, so she knows how fortunate she is to have a job.

We normally see Miss Baxter in the uniform of a lady's maid: black dress or blouse and skirt, her waistline dropped, hem mid-calf length, and her silhouette less corseted in line with 1920s style. On a day out to the seaside, she wears a relaxed smock-like top with a wide-brimmed straw hat, and there is an almost bohemian feel to her choice of clothing.

Miss Baxter takes great pleasure in visiting the French Riviera in *A New Era*, and she and Mr. Bates delight in the new sights and architecture around them. While she probably has few civilian clothes, she looks comfortable in the heat, wearing a loose-fitting, printed cotton gauze dress with a hem just below her knee. Further excitement is in store for her when She returns to Downton Abbey: she accepts Mr. Molesley's proposal of marriage, and we suspect new adventures are in store for the happy couple.

There is a simplicity and elegance to Miss Baxter's clothing, and she looks just as comfortable out of her lady's maid uniform.

HOLLYWOOD GUESTS

In *A New Era*, Hollywood stars descend on Downton Abbey to make an early talking picture. They and the film crew that accompanies them represent a world entirely different from the one inhabited by the Crawleys—one devoid of the formalities of aristocratic life. They look and behave very differently, and it was the job of costume, hair, and makeup to dress the houseguests in a way we've never seen at Downton.

Myrna Dalgleish, played by Laura Haddock, was the leading lady in the fictional film, and her look is something of a "visual shock" for everyone at Downton. "We wanted Myrna to have the feel of a quintessential Hollywood star," explains Anna Robbins. "She really shimmered, and we got to play with lots of amazing textures and textiles—with big sleeves, marabou feathers, and long trains that added to the drama of her character." To complement her platinum blonde hair (designed by hair and makeup designer Anne "Nosh" Oldham), Anna dressed Myrna in icy tones. "We used cool peaches and pinks, frosty turquoises and blues, and a palette that meant she popped in every setting. When you see her next to Mary, Edith, and Cora, her beauty clashes with theirs."

Myrna arrives at Downton Abbey wearing an icy, eau de Nil asymmetric dress with velvet coat trimmed in repurposed vintage fur, teamed with original 1920s silver shoes. The exaggerated shape was designed to heighten her boldness—everything about Myrna is bold and slightly brash, right down to the jewelry she wears.

Both Anna and Anne drew on references of movie idols from the period, including leading ladies Jean Harlow, Constance Bennett, and Greta Garbo.

Movie star Myrna Dalgleish wears a striking beaded Juliet cap (left), her look modeled on 1920s screen icon Greta Garbo (right).

Leading man Guy Dexter, played by Dominic West, also has a look of a Hollywood star, similar to real-life British actor Ronald Colman, who appeared in silent and talking movies in the 1920s and 1930s. Guy Dexter is a British actor living in Hollywood, which, as Anna Robbins explains, means "we were able to bring in a few American influences for what he wears. The cut of his jackets and the cloth of his suits are slightly different, and in one scene, he wears a double-breasted evening jacket, as the styles associated with the 1930s start to emerge, especially with the fashion-forward set in Hollywood."

Fictional director Jack Barber, played by Hugh Dancy, also represents a type rarely seen at Downton—a working professional. Anna Robbins dressed him in knitwear and trousers and waistcoats without suit jackets. "Barber has a relaxed confidence that balances the informality of his working wardrobe, often worn with rolled sleeves. And, in fact, a lot of the film crew sport an eclectic range of knitwear and separates that feels different from the classic three-piece suits we are accustomed to seeing on the gents above stairs."

Guy Dexter's look was based on real-life movie icon Ronald Colman (bottom left). Jack Barber's more relaxed style and hair was partly based on Bloomsbury artist Duncan Grant (bottom right).

CROWD SCENES: BROOKLANDS

Crowd scenes require extensive planning for the whole creative team behind *Downton Abbey*. The costume department must not only dress supporting artists but also ensure the principal artists stand out, with everything in shot capturing the mood of the scene. In season six, Henry Talbot competes in the new and exciting sport of motor racing in a scene that was actually filmed at the historic racing circuit of Goodwood in Sussex.

Henry and his fellow competitors are wearing racing coveralls in various shades and Lady Mary is in a striking red dress and sunglasses. The crowd we see in the stands were also carefully dressed by the costume team, as overseen by the crowd supervisor during filming. "We'd plan for a big set piece like this months ahead to ensure we had all the costumes we needed and the extra help required to dress the many supporting artists on filming days," explains Anna Robbins. "When it comes to designing for a crowd, every person you see should tell a story in terms of their age, social position, and who they're with. At Brooklands, the crowd was quite young and fashion-forward, and we wanted to inject some bright, bold summery colors."

Anna Robbins: "When designing for the Brooklands racing scene, we wanted to build an exciting, positive world with a colorful, modern-looking crowd."

CROWD SCENES: ROYAL PARADE

When dressing a crowd, the costume department would sometimes recycle clothing previously seen on principal actors. The caramel coat (opposite, top right) and green dress (opposite, bottom right), worn by supporting artists in the parade, are garments previously worn by Rosamund.

In the first *Downton* movie, we see a spectacular royal parade featuring Yorkshire Hussars on horseback, gun carriages, and hundreds of villagers waving flags and cheering. The costume department had to outfit not only the royal family, the Crawleys, and the yeomanry guards, but also the hundreds of supporting artists who lined the streets or milled around the raised dais in the village. It must ensure there is a good range of people, all authentically dressed in a way you might expect a crowd to look in a Yorkshire village in 1926. All supporting artists are outfitted according to character and status, ranging from well-to-do spectators in expensive-looking clothing to a fashionable twentysomething to a servant in her Sunday best to smartly dressed children—and, of course, they all wear hats for such an occasion.

The images opposite are photographs taken by continuity to ensure every supporting artist looked exactly the same over multiple days of filming. The royal parade took four days to shoot, which made these photographic records invaluable.

GUEST STARS

Over the years, an array of stars from the stage and screen have made appearances in *Downton Abbey*, ranging from Imelda Staunton and Dame Harriet Walter to Paul Giamatti and Richard E. Grant. While they are all renowned actors, they often make brief appearances in the series, so the audience needs to understand rapidly who they are and how they fit into the storyline.

"The guest stars might play a smaller role," explains Anna Robbins, "but their impact has to be equal to that of the principal players, although you'll have fewer costumes with which to tell their story. So the first costume you see them in has to say an awful lot—it's like a condensed form of costuming. It needs to be impactful, not necessarily in a bold way, but so you've encapsulated the essence of the character right from the outset, which you might then follow up with just two or three costumes." World famous opera singer Dame Kiri Te Kanawa (below) made a stunning guest appearance in series four of *Downton Abbey*, when she entertained house guests playing the real-life Australian soprano Dame Nellie Melba. Dominic West who played movie star Guy Dexter in *A New Era* instantly had the look of a Hollywood leading man, his suits, including his double-breasted evening jacket, looking a little more 1930s in style.

Guest star appearances in both the series and films include (clockwise from top left): Imelda Staunton (Maud Bagshaw); Nathalie Baye (Madame de Montmirail); Richard E. Grant (Simon Bricker); Dominic West (Guy Dexter); Dame Harriet Walter (Lady Shackleton); and Paul Giamatti (Harold Levinson).

CHILDREN

The nursery of *Downton Abbey* has, for much of the series, rung with the sound of children's voices. Sybbie, Tom and Sybil's daughter, and George, Mary and Matthew's son, are the eldest of the cousins. Then Marigold, Edith's daughter, comes to live at the house, followed by Caroline, Mary and Henry's daughter. Edith and Bertie's son, Peter, along with Tom and Lucy's newborn son are the latest additions to the family.

Filming laws mean that many of the children are played by twins: Oliver and Zac Barker double as George, and Eva and Karina Samms play Marigold. As a result, they required duplicate costumes, usually made by the costume department in a period style. George is often seen in a navy sailor suit (a traditional look for well-heeled children and popularized by Queen Victoria), a tailored tweed suit, or a mix of tie, shirt, and short trousers.

Sybbie, who is played by Fifi Hart, is more commonly seen in original items, the hemline of her dresses dropping as she grows older, with a 1920s-style dropped waist evident in some of her later pinafores. The children also wear period-appropriate knitwear, right down to the sleeve detail and wool color, as undertaken by knitters commissioned by the costume department.

Marigold sits with her grandmother and great aunt. Opposite are the various children featured in *Downton Abbey*, including Johnnie, Anna and Mr. Bates's son (in the second movie played by costume designer Anna Robbins's son Archer Robbins).

weldonowen

An imprint of Insight Editions

CEO Raoul Goff
VP Publisher Roger Shaw
Associate Publisher Amy Marr
VP Creative Chrissy Kwasnik
Art Director Allister Fein
Editorial Director Katie Killebrew
VP Manufacturing Alix Nicholaeff
Sr Production Manager Joshua Smith

Produced by Weldon Owen
P.O. Box 3088
San Rafael, CA 94912
www.weldonowen.com

ISBN: 978-1-68188-522-3

Printed in China.
10 9 8 7 6 5 4 3 2 1

Weldon Owen wishes to thank the following people for their generous support in producing this book: Rachel Markowitz, Elizabeth Parson, and Sharon Silva.

Weldon Owen also wishes to thank Gareth Neame, Charlotte Fay, and Nion Hazell at Carnival Films; Megan Startz and Melissa Rodriguez at NBCUniversal; Amy Rivera at Focus Features; and Annabel Merullo and Daisy Chandley at Peters Fraser + Dunlop.

FROM THE AUTHOR

It has been such a delight to talk to everyone involved with the costumes of *Downton Abbey* and I owe a great deal of thanks to the costume designers Susannah Buxton, Rosalind Ebbutt, Caroline McCall, and Anna Mary Scott Robbins. Their expertise, creative vision, and passion for what they do is extraordinary. I owe particular thanks to Anna Robbins, who gave so much of her time to this book and passed on invaluable knowledge and insight. Over the years the costume designers have worked closely with an array of talented people, and they would like to pass on particular thanks to John Bright at Cosprop, Richard Green at Angels, Sean Barrett, Sophie Millard, Chris Kerr, Bentley & Skinner, and Maja Meschede. The author would also like to thank Gareth Neame and Charlotte Fay at Carnival Films; Roger Shaw, Amy Marr, and Allister Fein at Weldon Owen; and Annabel Merullo and Daisy Chandley at Peters Fraser + Dunlop.

© Victoria and Albert Museum, London: Heather Firbank (93)

Alamy: Queen Alexandra, Queen Mary with George V (62), Madeleine Vionnet sketches (117), George Barbier illustration (126), King George V and Queen Mary (159), Queen Mary & Princess Elizabeth (163), vintage tennis photo (199), female and male race car drivers (201), 1920s bride (222), Livery sketch (247), and Ronald Coleman and Duncan Grant (261),

Anna Robbins: cloth background (22-23), Cora's blouse (38), Cora's Royal Ball dress (40), Cora's Royal Ball dress material (41), Edith's afternoon tea sketch (50), Mary's afternoon tea sketch (53), Violet's dress material (70), Violet's Royal Ball dress (83), Mary's Royal Ball dress (85), Lady Mary's outfit sketch (110), Mary's night dress (122), Edith's Palazzo pants sketch (141), Queen Mary's dress (161), Mary's silk pajama sketch (179), Tuppence Middleton wedding dress fitting (222), cloth background (224-225), livery costume sketch (246), and supporting artists (267)

All third-party trademarks are the property of their respective owners.

ABOUT THE AUTHOR

Emma Marriott is the author of more than fifteen high-profile popular histories and other non-fiction books, including the last two companions to the *Downton Abbey* movies, *The World of Vanity Fair*, and *The World of Poldark*. A former in-house editor at Pan Macmillan in London, she lives in Bedfordshire, England.